Images In Ochre

THE ART AND CRAFT OF THE KUNWINJKU

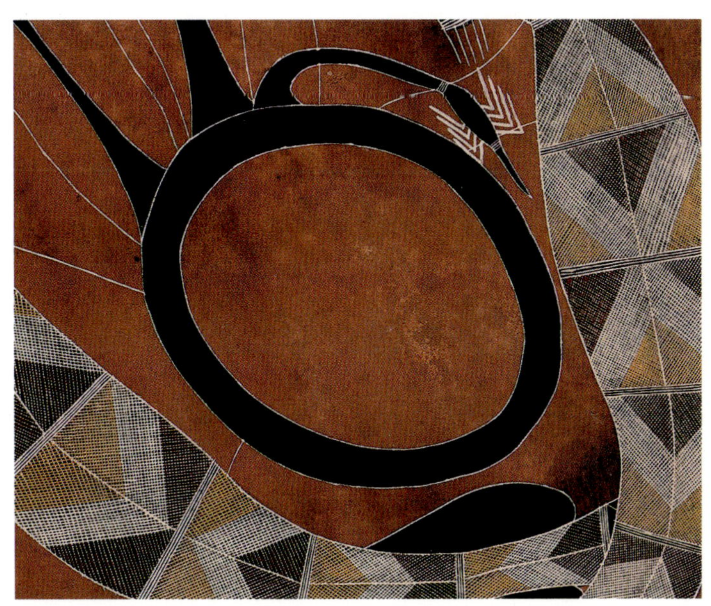

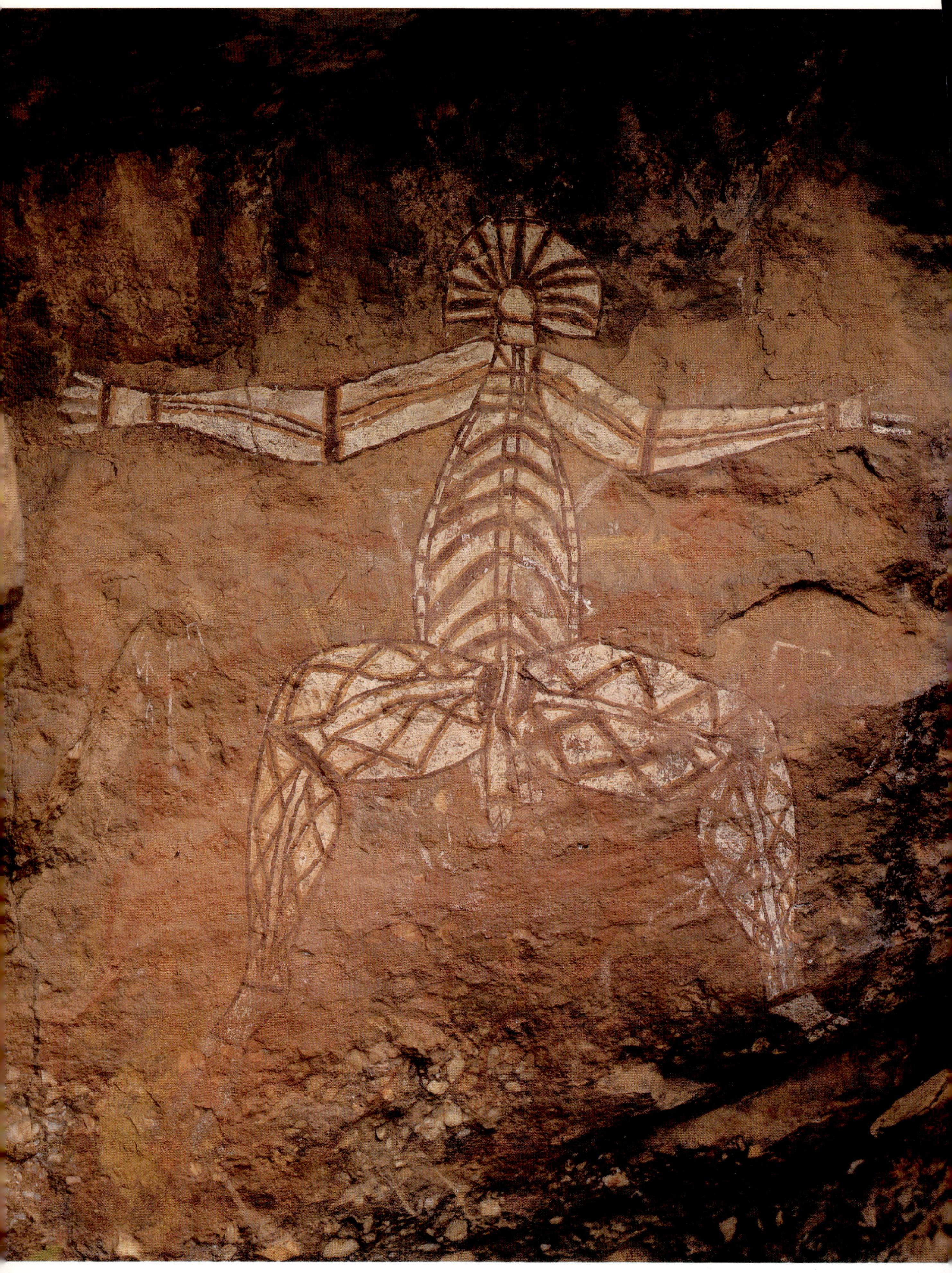

Images In Ochre

THE ART AND CRAFT OF THE KUNWINJKU

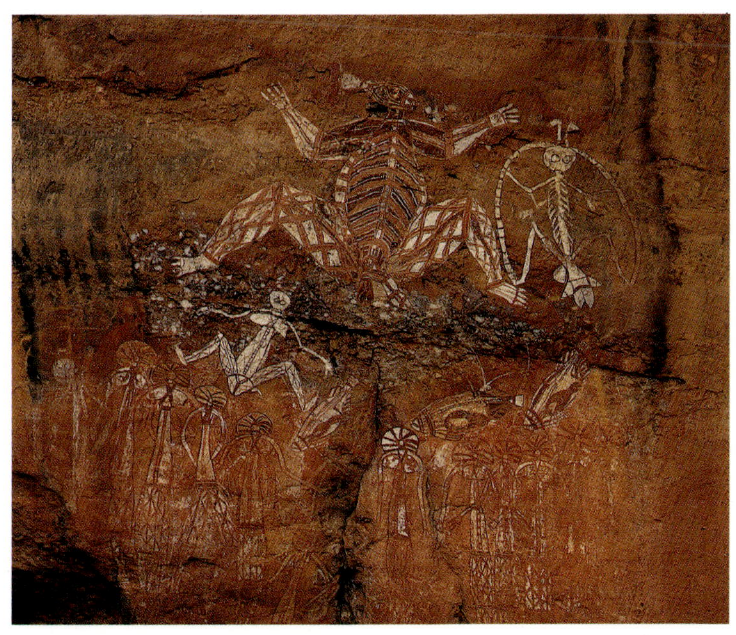

Adrian Parker

Photography by Adrian Parker & Selwyn Horsnell

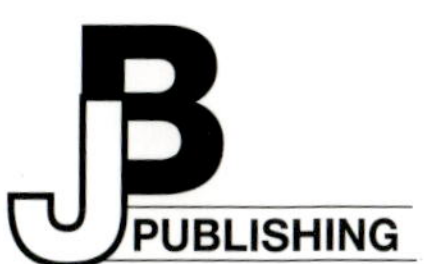

Glossary

Binninj	Aboriginal people, specifically Aboriginal man
Bondock	woomera
Dhuwa	one of two main skin groups
Djang	sacred
Dreamtime	creation period
Ginga	saltwater crocodile
Gunumeleng	October-December, the pre-monsoonal period
Gurrung	August-September
Kunwinjku	people of western Arnhem Land
Mearu	fighting stick
Mimi	non-physical entity or spirit
Namarnkol	barramundi
Namarrkon	'Lightning Man'
Ngalkunburriyaymi	female Rainbow Serpent
Ngalyod	Rainbow Serpent
Rangga	sacred objects
Rarrk	cross-hatching
Waramurungundj	Earth Mother
Yawk Yawk	freshwater mermaid
Yekke	April-May, burn-off season
Yingarna	mother Rainbow Serpent (also *Waramurungundj*)
Yirridja	one of two main skin groups

This edition published in 2004 by
J.B. Publishing
P.O. Box 118, Marleston, South Australia 5033

First published in 1997 by Kangaroo Press
an imprint of Simon and Schuster (Australia) Pty Ltd.
Reprinted 2000

ISBN 0 86417 892 1
Designed by Kerry Klinner
Produced by Phoenix Offset, Hong Kong

Front and back cover, pages 1,2,3 and 5 and all photographic reproductions of art
by Selwyn Horsnell (S.H.)

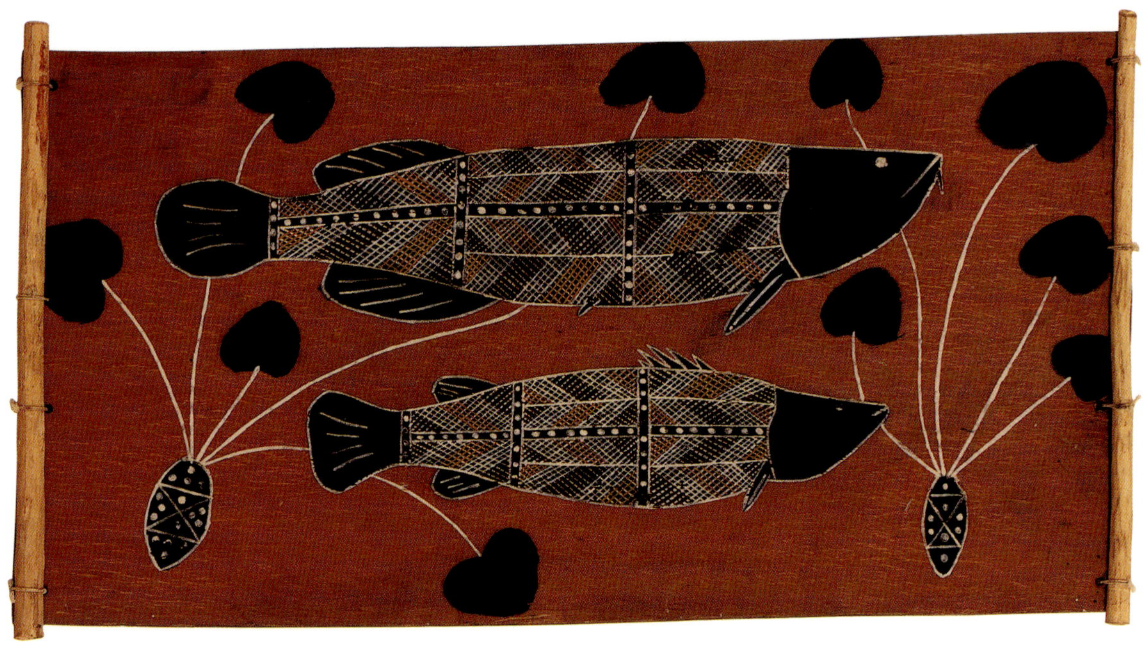

Contents

For more than two centuries, Anglo-Australians have misunderstood the original occupants of this continent. In the main the misunderstanding has been deliberate and baleful, for ours is a nation built on the pastoral, agricultural and mineral wealth generated from expropriated land. Many, from philanthropist to scholar, have sincerely endeavoured to gain insight into the physical and conceptual universe of Australia's first peoples, but generally it must be said that they too were bound to misinterpret. The problem is that Europeans view Aboriginal people through lenses poorly focussed to appreciate the complexities of lifestyles and cosmologies so intrinsically different to their own.

The historical record shows that Aboriginal peoples have been far more receptive. In the dialogue between cultures, they have been the more enthusiastic, the more flexible and the more insightful. This is clearly borne out by the experiences of Adrian Parker. He has learnt much during his sojourn in the Kakadu region because he has found such eager teachers. He describes his Kunwinjku friends as 'culturally generous'. This book is a product of goodwill.

Foreword

For the Kunwinjku people of Kakadu and west Arnhem Land, art is a principal medium for promoting cross-cultural awareness. While recent contact with Anglo-Australians has stimulated some changes in the method, purpose and presentation of traditional art, it remains a most potent and instructive expression of cultural and spiritual realities. Art has been used for thousands of generations to vitalise beliefs and values and, especially, to impart them to the young. Now, they extend a little of the same privilege and opportunity to non-Aboriginals.

This rare and enchanting style of art profoundly intrigues non-Aboriginals, so laden with meanings they can never fully appreciate but abounding in aesthetic qualities that are universally admired. Such is the eagerness of these artists to have their works enjoyed and understood by others that by producing art for public sale they are consciously and sincerely proffering a spirit of partnership. It is but one means by which we might, finally, begin to comprehend those who understand this land better than anyone.

David A. Roberts

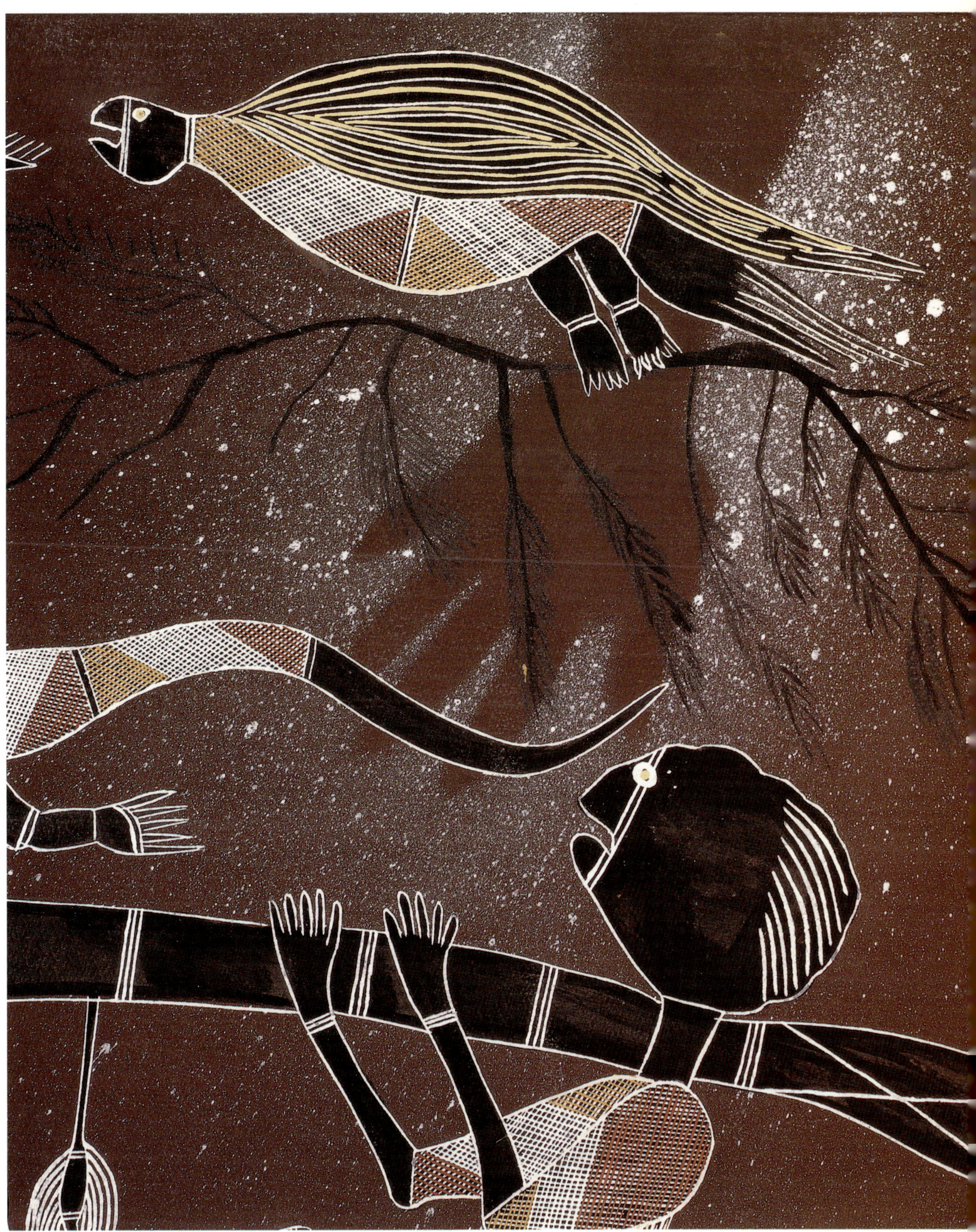

S.H.

In May 1995 I came to Kakadu National Park for a six-week art exhibition at the Gagudju Crocodile Hotel in Jabiru. I had been painting for some years since completing a degree in history and sociology at Newcastle University, NSW. Anthropology featured in my education, but reading and studying ill prepared me for my first meetings with the Kunwinjku. Moreover, I quickly realised that a few days in the bush with these people could teach me more than three years of study.

My initial bonding with the local men was through the common link of art. They were amazed and amused that I chose to paint realistic images of their environment and people. In turn, I was intrigued by the subject matter and techniques of the *Binninj* people. Eventually, they offered me the opportunity to observe and learn traditional painting techniques. They told me stories and related cultural information. With much enthusiasm and considerable patience, they also taught me to play the didgeridoo.

Dedication

I realised how culturally generous the traditional owners were. It was not important that I was non-Aboriginal. What was important was that I am a man and they could therefore show me men's things. Gender plays a strong role in Aboriginal society. The roles of each sex are clearly defined. They dominate one's life and permeate all aspects of it, including ceremony, knowledge, work, hobbies and interests. When I quizzed the men on how pandanus palm is woven, they received my questions with marked disinterest. 'That's woman's business', they told me, as we searched for more stringybark saplings to make didgeridoos.

The manufacture and playing of didgeridoos is also gender based. Women are not allowed to play, nor do they aspire to. They believe that if a woman plays the didgeridoo she may become pregnant without knowing who the father is. However, any man, regardless of his culture, is allowed to play and he will receive much encouragement from the Kunwinjku men. Most traditional stories about the discovery and creation of the didgeridoo are based on the phallus; similarities between the physiology of a man's penis and a long hollow log are common.

This book is a product of my experiences with Aboriginal people in Kakadu and West Arnhem Land. It would not have been possible without the blessing, encouragement and assistance of my Kunwinjku friends. To them, the following pages and my thanks are dedicated. Special thanks to Alex Nganjmirra, Danny Djorlom, Chris Ngaboy, John Lemibanda, Abraham Dakgalawuy, Thompson Nganjmirra, Trevor Nganjmirra, Mark Nadjongorle, Joshua Bangar, David Cameron, Clancy, and my many friends. Thanks also to those at the Gagudju Crocodile Hotel, and to Selwyn Horsnell, a gifted professional photographer. Thanks also to my friend David Roberts for his advice and guidance.

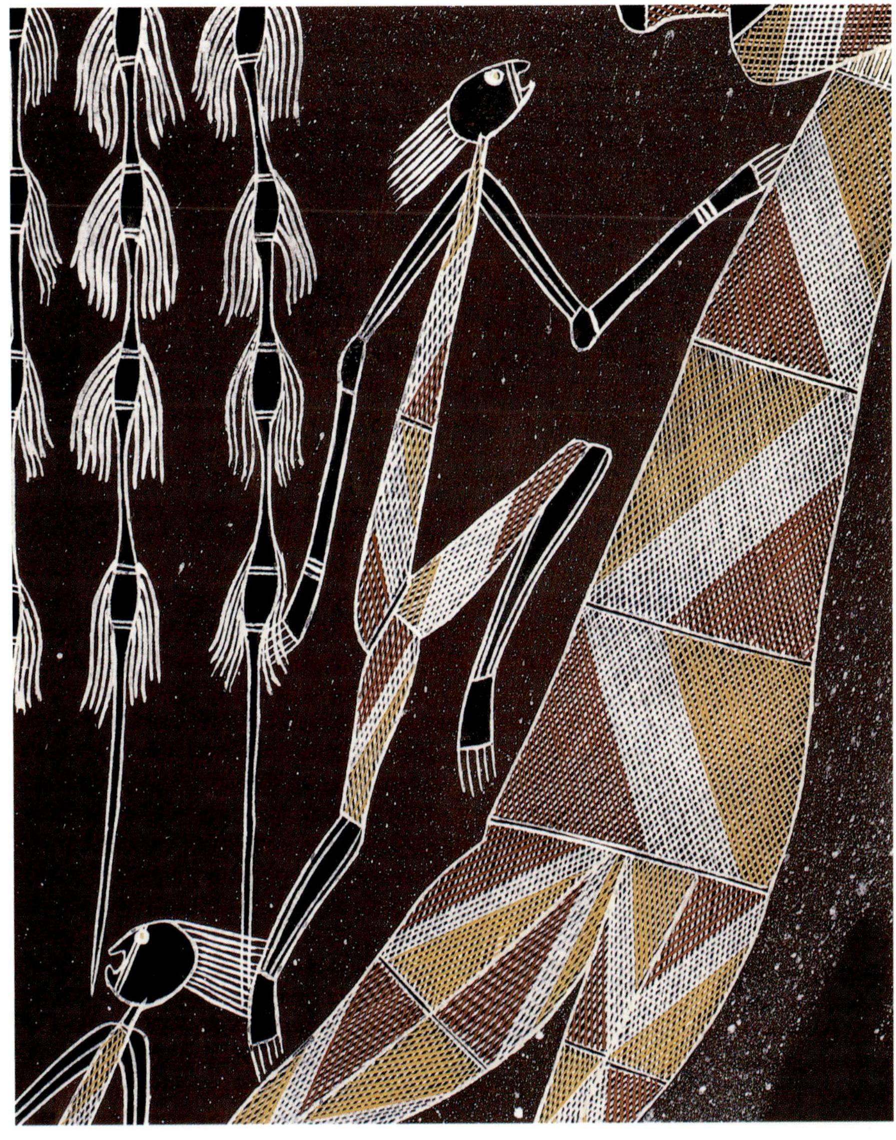

S.H.

Two hours drive east of Darwin, the capital of the Northern Territory, lies Kakadu National Park. With approximately 20 000 square km under World Heritage listing, it is Australia's largest National Park, leased under strict conditions from the traditional Aboriginal owners. To the east of Kakadu lies Arnhem Land, 94 000 square km of Aboriginal land, spanning the north-eastern portion of the Top End, with a population of about 6 000. Small scattered townships like Oenpelli (*Gunbalanya*) and some mining areas like Jabiru constitute the major developments that have taken place in these areas.

The land is crisscrossed by rivers and streams that have their source in the escarpment country. Beneath the escarpments lay vast flood plains created by thousands of years of monsoonal rain. The rivers wind their way through low-lying savannah woodlands, dispersing over extensive coastal mudflats before emptying into the Van Dieman Gulf. It is highly fertile country, rich in natural resources and abounding in wildlife.

Introduction

The climate of the Top End of Australia is governed by two main seasons, the Wet and the Dry. Animal populations, the land and its appearance change with the seasons. From mid-December to March, the Wet–the monsoon season–causes rivers and waterways to breach their banks and flood the plains, reuniting billabongs and waterholes. Dormant bushlands come alive with new life and tropical growth. Speargrass shoots up to three metres in height, making the bush dense and impassable.

When the rains cease, the bush and landscape slowly begin to dry. Billabongs become independent of their neighbours, capturing crocodiles, fish and other marine life within their banks. Eventually these bodies of water become the sustenance not only of the life they contain, but also of the animals and birds that inhabit the bush around them.

When the winds are dry and the spear grass becomes less impenetrable, it is *Yekke*; time for the 'burn-off'. The grass and dry undergrowth is systematically set alight. Fire moves swiftly through the bush, turning fallen trees, branches and

dry brush into dust, charcoal and smouldering
stumps. The crowns of the trees remain
beyond the reach of licking flames. The rich
greens of a few months earlier are replaced by
hues of deep yellow, red and black. Smoke fills
the northern air for weeks on end.

During August and September
(*Gurrung*) the waterholes continue to recede
and life becomes difficult for the flora and
fauna that rely on them. Fertile pools
eventually become wastelands of dry,
parched mud. Below the cracked surface,
turtles and frogs await new rains. It seems
that the Dry will continue forever, until a

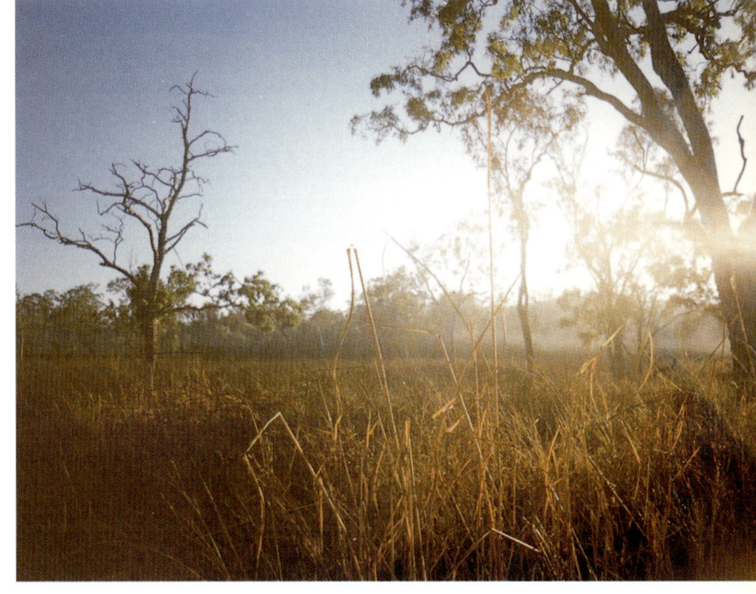

ABOVE: *Yekke*

BELOW: *A Jabiru searching for food*

brief period of windy days in September signals the beginning of 'the buildup'.
During the pre-monsoonal period (*Gunumeleng*), humidity soars while huge
towers of cloud and electrical storms foretell that within weeks life-renewing
rain will come again. During this period, days are oppressively hot and sticky,
until at last violent storms bring the rains that revitalise the life-cycle of the
ancient land and its inhabitants. Constant seasonal changes guide the life of
the Aboriginal people who subsist within this environment.

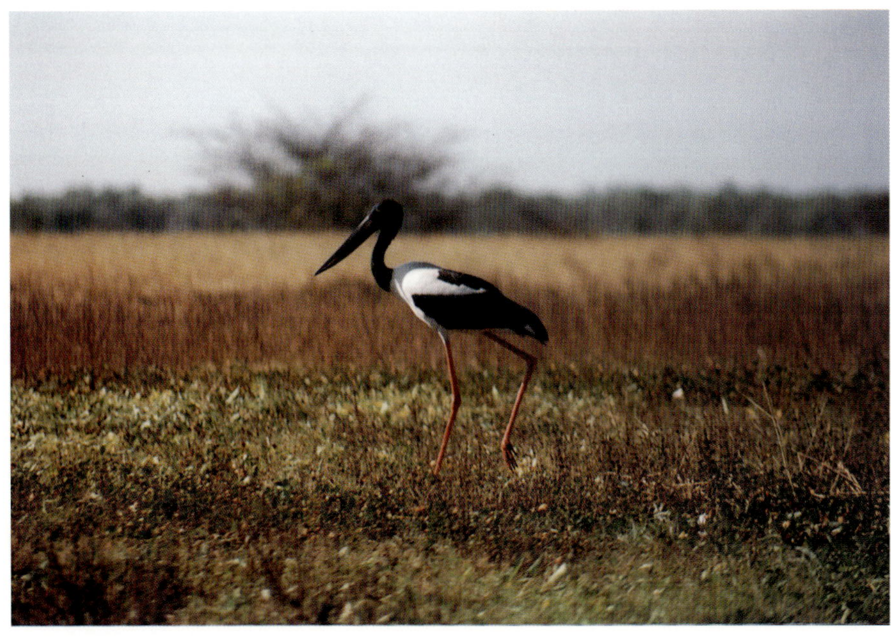

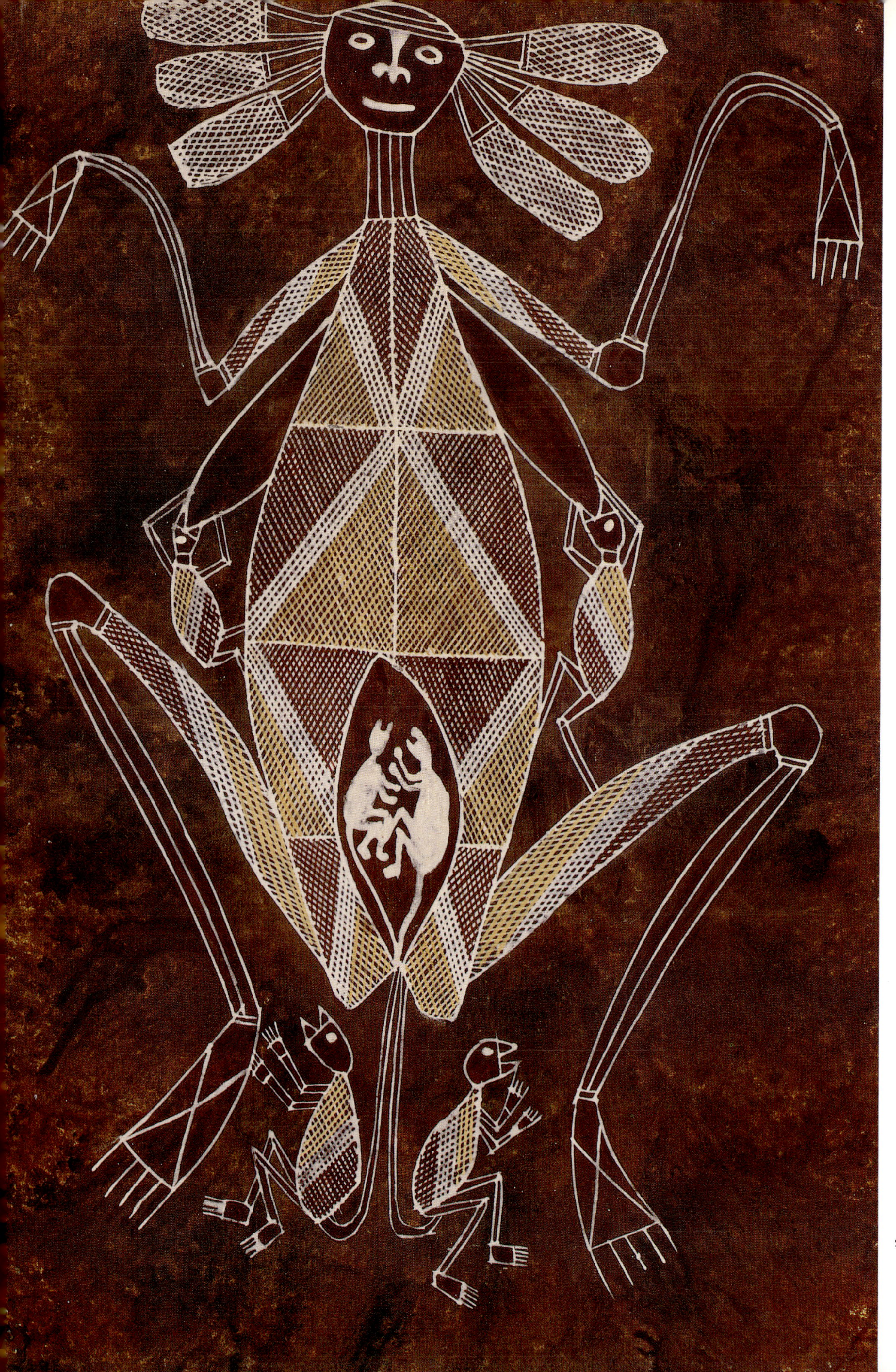

S.H.

At university in the late 1980s I was taught that Aboriginal people had occupied Australia for around 12 000 years, having migrated to the continent from the north at times when the sea levels were low enough to form land bridges. By the early 1990s, the recognised period of occupation had been extended to 60 000 years. However, recent archaeological digs in the Kimberley region suggest that the period of occupation may be closer to 120 000 years.

To the Aborigines, these dates are superfluous. They understand that they originated here and that they have occupied the land since time immemorial. In local history (as told by Danny Djorlom), the people were born of *Yingarna*, the mother Rainbow Serpent who metamorphosed into *Waramurungundj* (the Earth Mother). She came from the north across the sea, creating many islands, peoples and languages. She entered the mainland south of Croker Island, giving birth to the Rainbow Serpents *Ngalyod*, her first born

Images In Ochre

son, and *Ngalkunburriyaymi*, the female Rainbow Serpent. They were followed by other Creation beings like *Luma Luma* and the *Yawk Yawk* sisters. They moved across the country creating the land, rivers, hills, people, flora and fauna. *Waramurungundj* then headed south, never to return. Other beings entered the land to sleep when Creation was complete.

The paths travelled by the ancestral beings are well known today. They are generally referred to as 'songlines'. Today, descendants maintain various sites regarded as sacred (*djang*), performing specific rites and rituals relating to the beings and sites that are important to each particular clan. Though clan members will have the same country in common, individuals call that area 'my country'. Connections between land and spirituality are cooperative and shared, but individuals also maintain highly personalised links.

It is believed that art has been a form of expression for Aboriginal people since their arrival on this continent. The discovery of an ochre pencil in the Kakadu region in late 1995, at a site shown to non-Aboriginal

This painting is of *Waramurungundj* (Earth Mother), a metamorphosis of *Yingarna*, the Mother Rainbow Serpent. According to Danny Djorlom, 'on her way she gave birth to many islands and people. *Ngalyod* and the creator beings are her children. The dilly bags around her head are to carry food.'

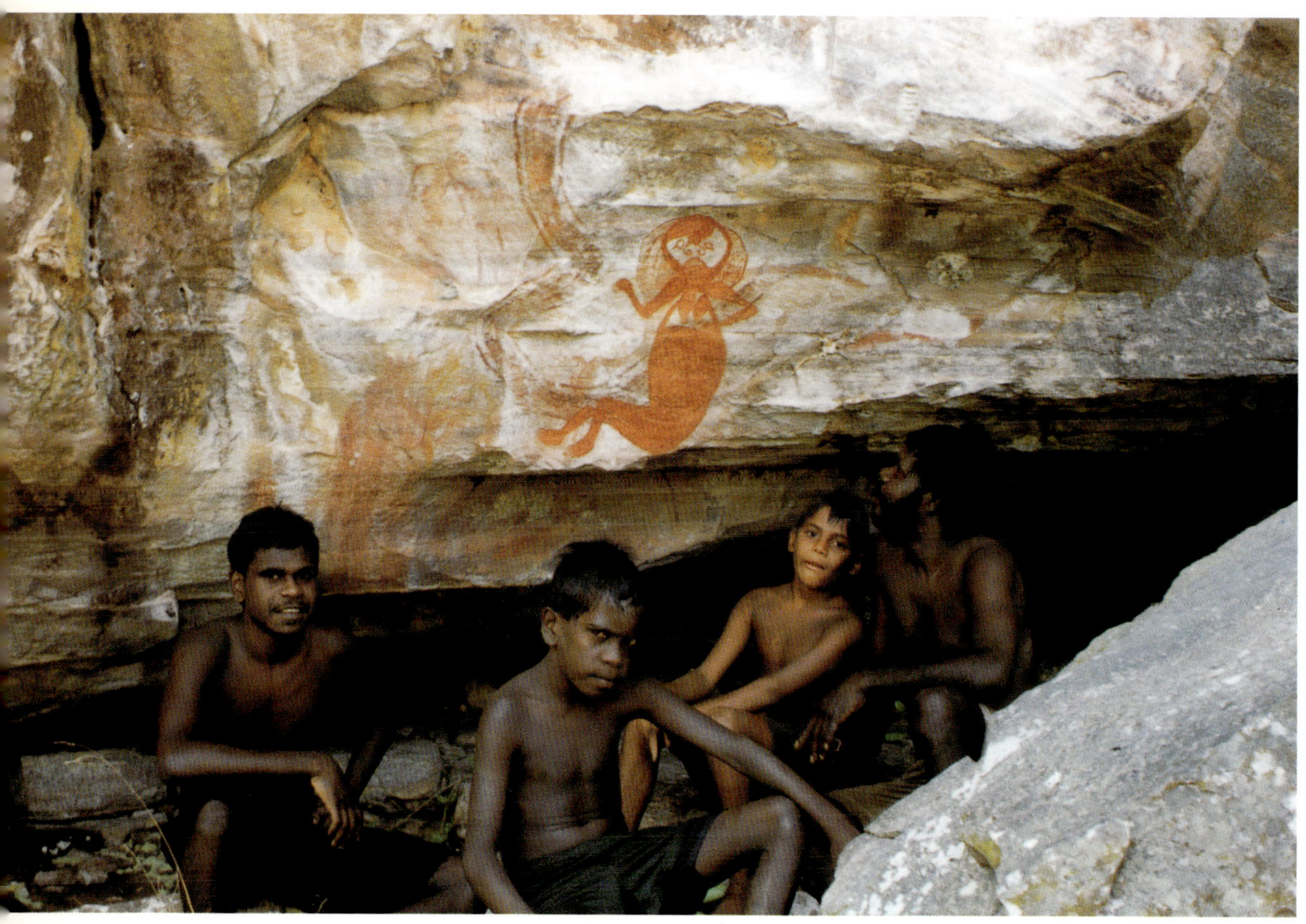

Australians for the first time by a local elder, suggests that the tradition of producing art from ochre and charcoal is much older than previously believed. In any event, Aboriginal art could be considered the oldest continuous tradition of artistic expression. Painting traditions continue across the northern parts of Australia as they have done for thousands of generations.

In recent years a new generation of Kunwinjku artists has come to the fore. Traditions thousands of years old have been taught to them, and as young men they are now the main practitioners. A wealth of vibrant, talented artists now exists. Some individuals are known internationally, and there are many others who have the potential to be.

In contrast to shelter paintings, both Australian desert canvas paintings and works on paper now produced in the Kakadu and west Arnhem Land regions are recent innovations. Before and since the introduction of paper, the Kunwinjku and Gagudju people regularly practised the tradition of painting on bark. Paintings of both tribes have similar styles and subject matter, reflected indirectly through story, marriage and language links. Beween areas such as the Kimberley or east Arnhem Land, art styles vary distinctly.

Traditionally, the purpose of painting has been to help convey knowledge of ancestral beings by animating oral history. This is done in conjunction with song, dance and sacred objects. Themes and subject matter are handed down from generation to generation (usually from father to son), although each artist will have his own individual style. Artists do not sign their work; their individual style is their trademark. From a young age an apprenticeship system exists. Children are not only taught hunting, tracking and gathering skills but also painting skills and the ancestral stories represented in the paintings.

Through his work the artist expresses his degree of initiation and knowledge. Although the uninitiated may view paintings, the symbolism and knowledge cannot be revealed. Like stories, painting styles can vary slightly from clan to clan. Even when painting for public sale the artist is reaffirming his ancestral links.

A less frequently practised form of art is sorcery painting, in which the artist depicts the subject succumbing to various intent. Figures can be dismembered, disembowelled, or made to suffer torment, discomfort and misfortune. A typical reason for producing this type of painting is to punish marital infidelity. Earlier this century, however, Christian missionaries effectively eradicated this practice.

A hand stencil painted by Alex Nganjmirra's father

One ancestoral being which is painted regularly and is typical of the west Arnhem Land and Kakadu regions is the *Mimi* spirit. A nonphysical being, the *Mimi* resides in the country where flood plains and escarpment meet, generally in cracks or small caves. Artistically they are represented as small human-like figures. Culturally, they can be constructive, teaching knowledge and skills, or destructive and mischievous. They are also used to explain irregular occurences or the existence of slightly unusually phenomena in the landscape.

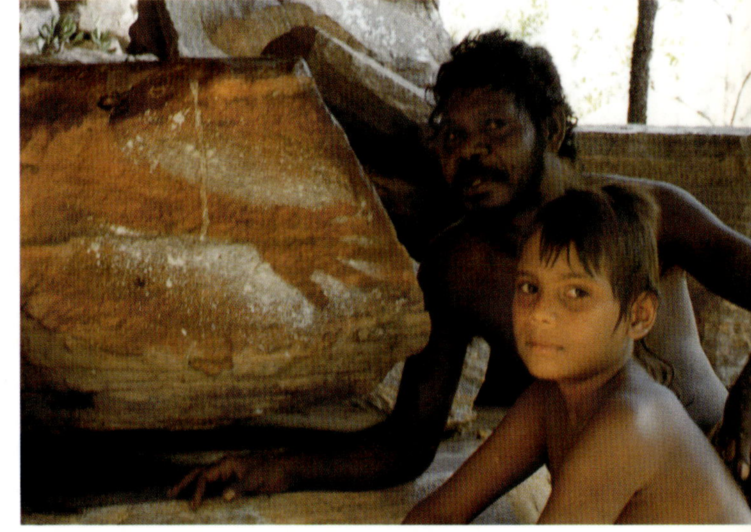

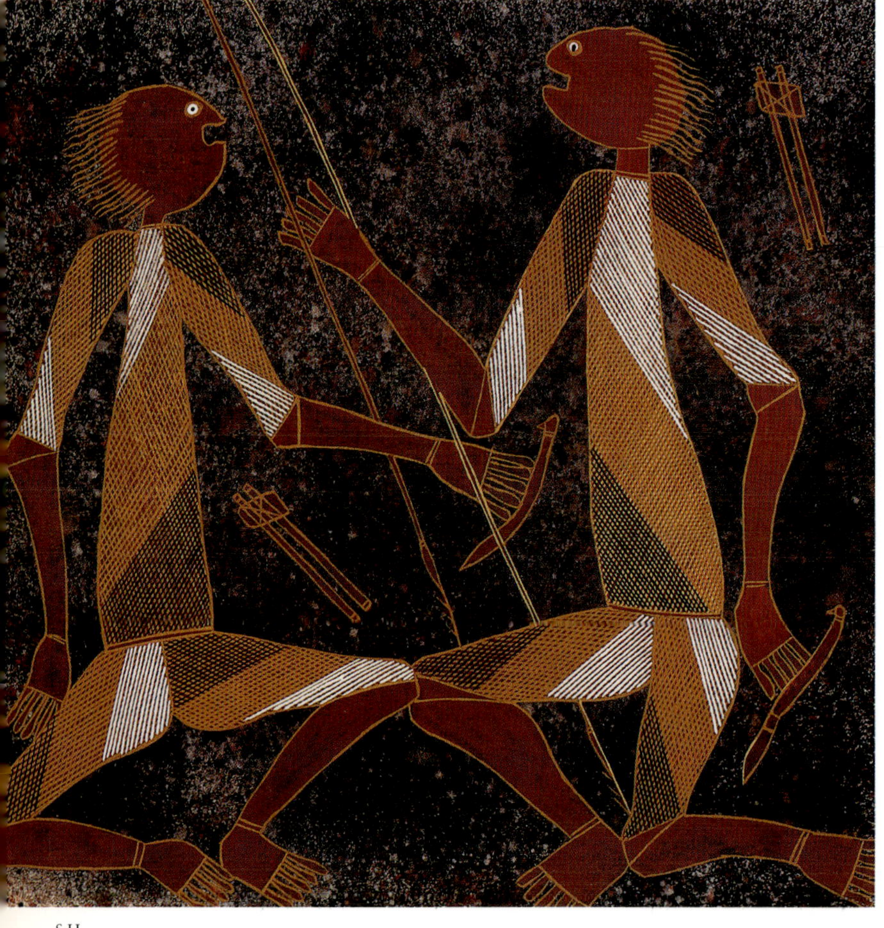

S.H.

Another popular theme for artists are items of importance in day-to-day living, for instance foodstuffs like barramundi and wallaby (which for some are *djang*) and depictions of the hunt, and items used for hunting and gathering.

Sleeping beings like *Ngalyod* and *Ngalkunburriyaymi* will awaken to punish negligence or travesty. Thus ancient oral and painted stories can be adapted to explain contemporary occurances. For instance, the recent disappearance of two white fishermen in the Magela area is explained in local knowledge by the belief that the fishermen were making excessive noise, waking up the Rainbow Serpent, which then ate them.

This story illustrates the elasticity and evolving nature of traditional culture. Contemporary themes reinforce and illustrate, for a younger generation, beliefs that are thousands of years old.

ABOVE: Payback, *by Alex Nganjmirra, 52 x 51 cm*
The Kunwinjku punish the breaking of tribal law in different ways, and as in Western society, punishment fits the crime. For *Binninj* people, minor punishment can be the payment of a fine in money or foodstuffs, while the most extreme punishment is death. A well-known crime for which the death penalty exists is disclosure of ceremonial secrets. In this painting a perpetrator is being speared in the leg for adultery.

OPPOSITE: *Dancing Figures, Nourlangie Rock*

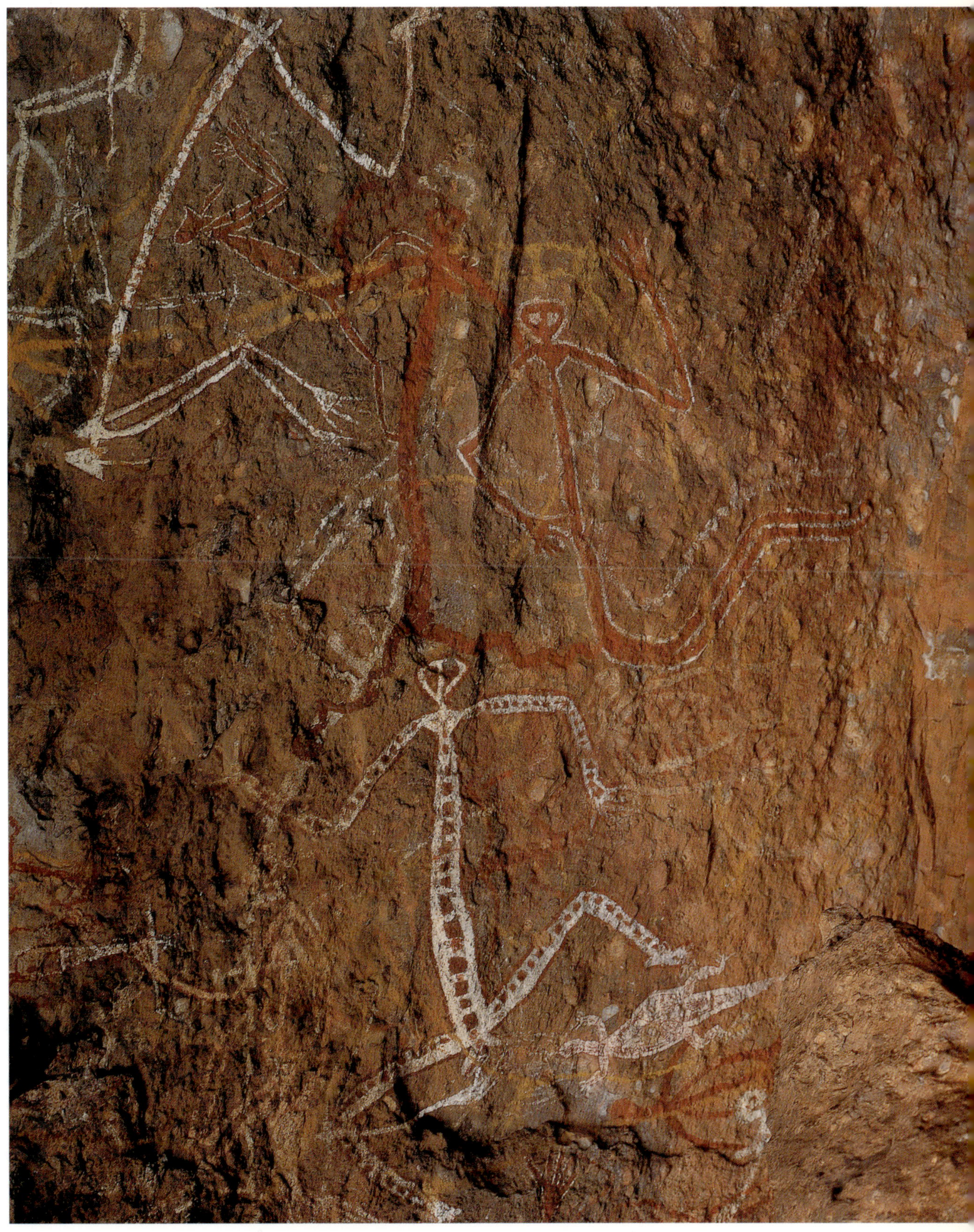

S.H.

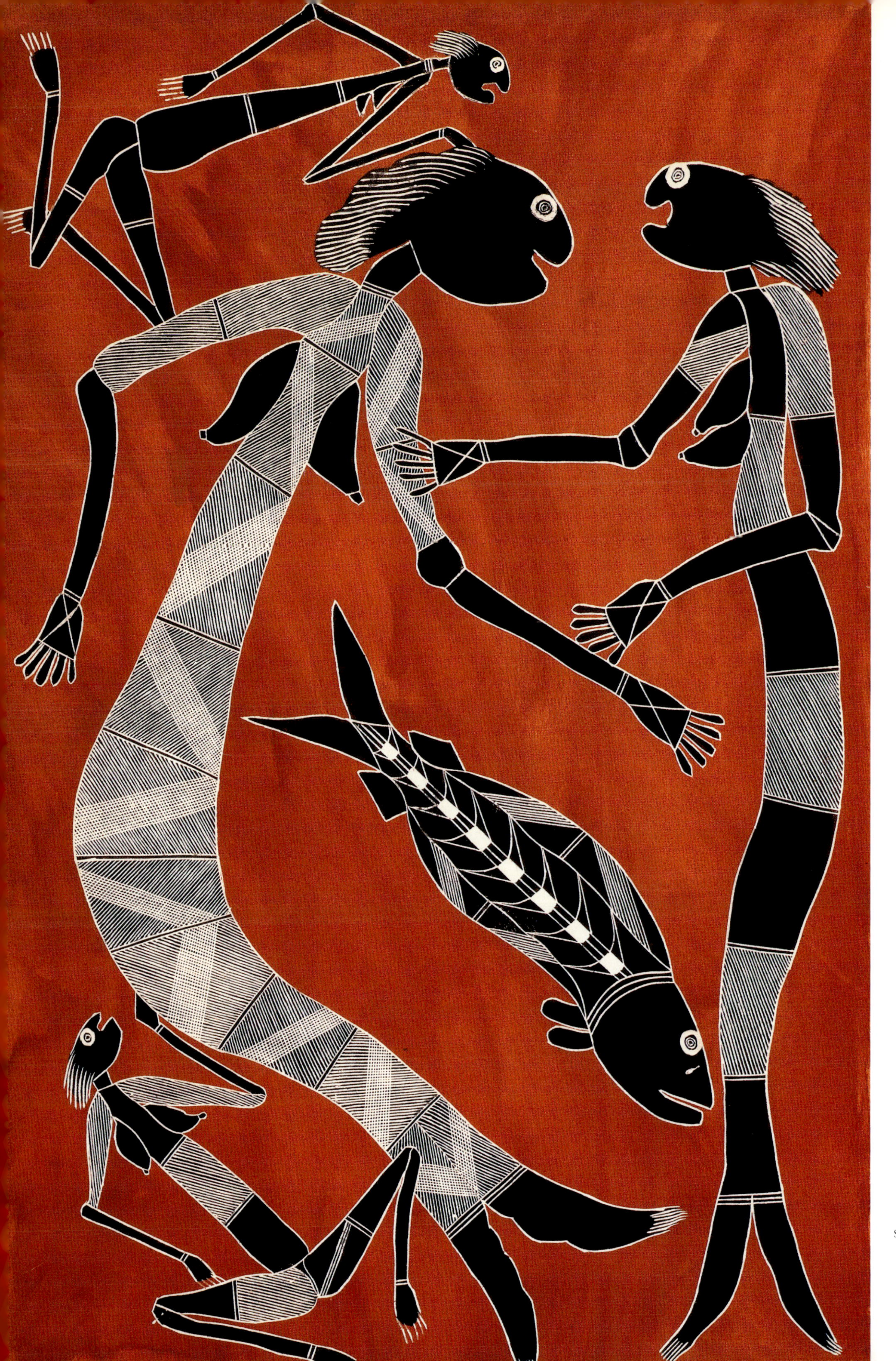

S.H.

*B*inninj, or Aboriginal society, is rigidly structured. Skin groups exist for many important reasons. The two main groups are *Dhuwa* and *Yirridja*. People must marry outside their skin group and thus their clan. This helps curb intermarriage and creates harmony between clans. Skin groups perform different ceremonial roles and accordingly are taught different laws. Certain areas of land are also the territory of the different skin groups. East Kakadu and Oenpelli are *Yirridja* country, while the area between Oenpelli and Kakadu is shared by *Dhuwa* and *Yirridja*. Low country is *Dhuwa* land, though of course exceptions do exist. While Kakadu is generally referred to as Gagudju country, and west Arnhem Land as Kunwinjku country, many

Skin Groups

Kunwinjku now reside in Kakadu and have done so for generations. Thus, contemporary Kunwinjku art is synonymous with both west Arnhem Land and Kakadu.

After initiation, the subject matter that an artist is allowed to paint increases. The artist is taught the stories, meanings and laws contained within the subject. Certain subjects are the domain of *Dhuwa*, others *Yirridja*. The artist expresses his skin group via his painting technique. The *rarrk* painted by *Dhuwa* is much thicker and more widely spaced than the fine, closely knit *rarrk* of the *Yirridja*.

Traditionally, heavy penalties applied for using the incorrect painting style. The artist was also not allowed to paint his personal Dreaming, though it could be painted by a cousin or near relative. Today, many artists do paint their own Dreaming without penalty, especially if the works are for private sale rather than cultural purposes. Stealing or using another clan's design is prohibited.

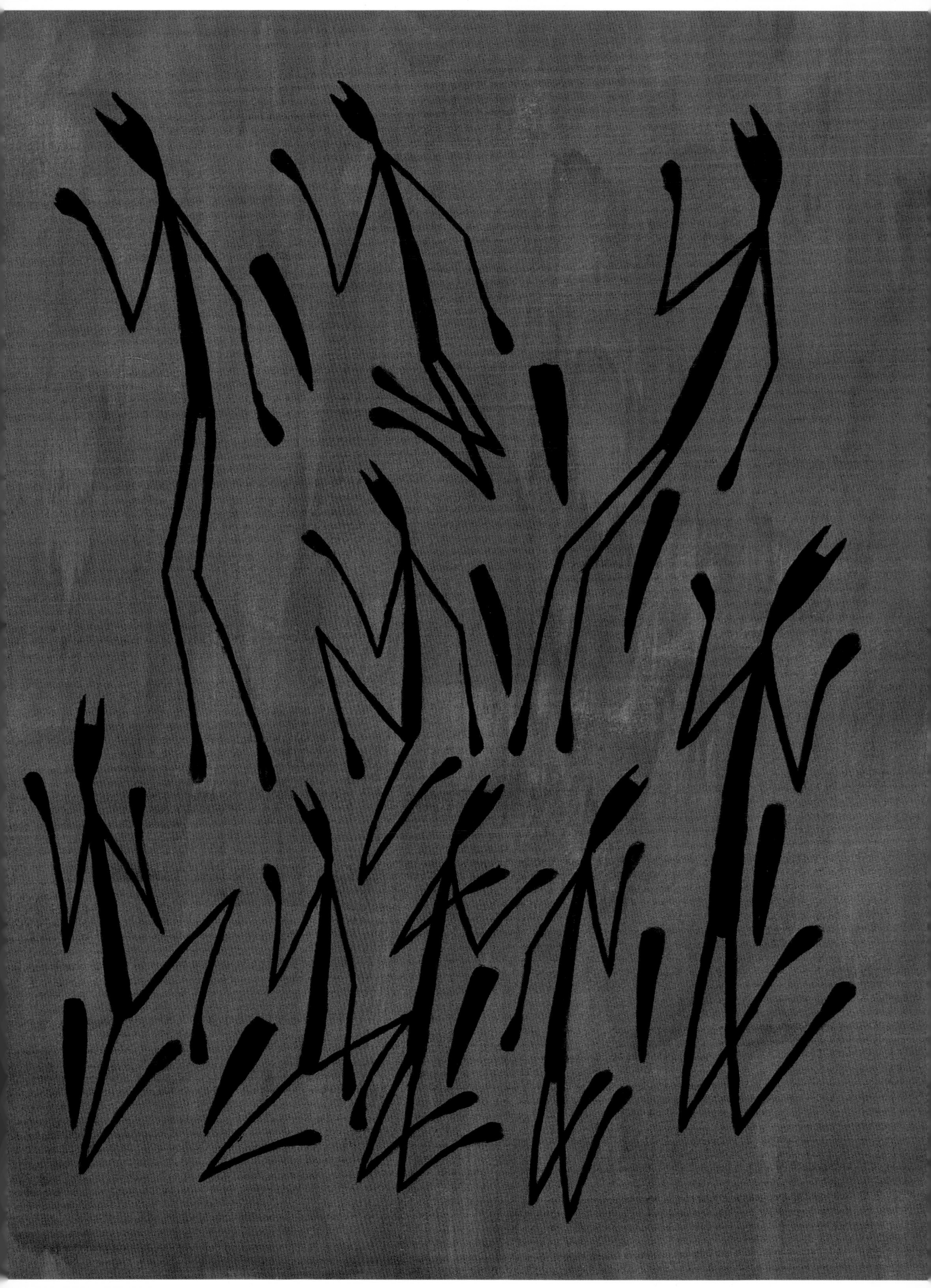

Traditionally, painting has been the domain of men, though occasionally women artists can be found. Techniques of ochre application have varied little over the years, although various distinct painting styles exist. *Rarrk* (cross-hatching) may be crisscrossed or parallel lines, and sometimes a combination of the two. Monochrome figures and images that contain no *rarrk* are common at rock-art sites, and are still painted occasionally.

OCHRE

Ochre is a naturally occurring pigment used for surface and body painting. Ochres generally correspond to the 'earth' colours in Western acrylics and oil paints–yellow ochres, light reds and white. Charcoal from campfires is used for black.

Painting Techniques

Ochre can be found throughout the bush. The best collecting sites are where erosion has occurred, or in the vicinity of waterways. Increasingly, pigments are collected from the coastal regions near Darwin, where red, white and yellow are readily available along the cliffs and beaches.

Traditionally, gathering rights for the colours were based on skin group. *Dhuwa* gathered red and white, while *Yirridja* gathered yellow and black. The colours were then exchanged or traded between the skin groups. This practice, however, is waning and most artists will collect all colours despite their skin group.

Ochre is still the medium of choice for the Kunwinjku artists, over acrylic and other commercially available paints. It has several features that

Opposite: Monochrome *Mimi Spirits and Dilly Bags, by Chris Ngaboy, 48 x 61 cm*

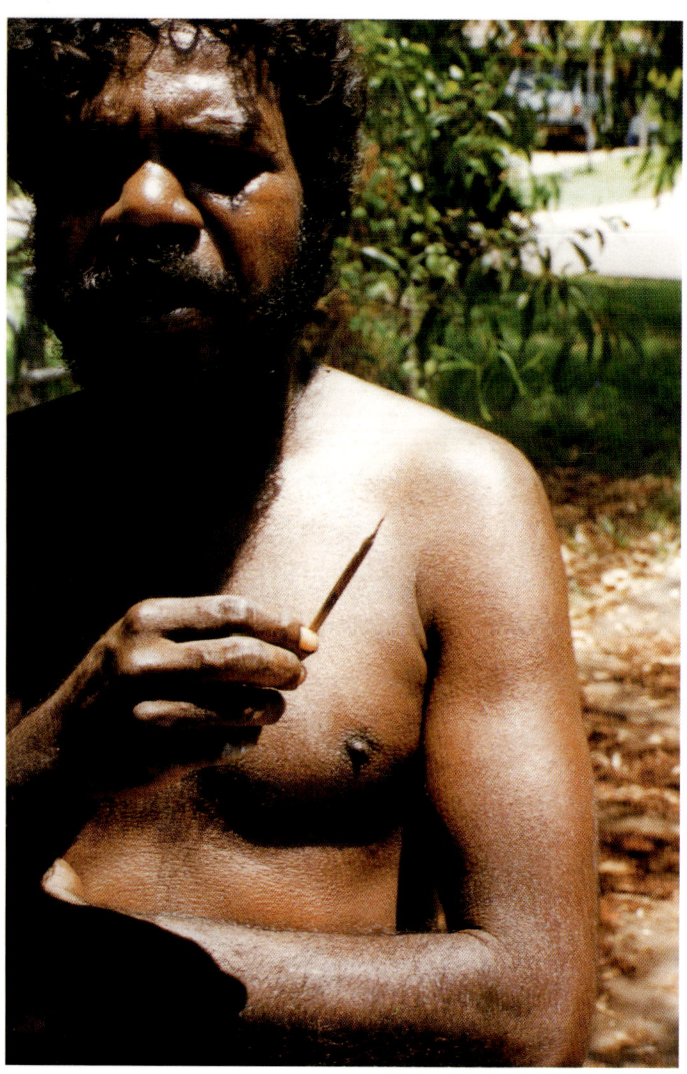

Alex Nganjmirra with a reed brush used for crosshatching

mass-produced paints lack. Firstly, it is long lasting and does not fade with time, as do many manufactured pigments. Ochre also has a unique, pastel-like texture when applied. Furthermore, it costs nothing.

In its natural state ochre is dense and rock-like. To prepare as a pigment, both ochre and charcoal are ground or crushed into a fine powder. Water and a binding agent are added to give a paint-like fluidity. Traditionally the binding agent was animal blood, beeswax, egg white (used in gouache paints) or plant-bulb resin; without it, ochre will flake or rub off easily. Today, however, PVA glues are widely used as a substitute.

When painting, the artist usually sits or squats on the ground. The colours are ground close by, preferably on cement, rock or other hard surfaces. White is usually kept separate in a lid or tobacco tin; like most white pigments it is easily discoloured. The ground pigments are mixed with a roughly equal amount of water and 1:4 binding agent. When smooth, they are ready to apply.

BRUSHES

Brushes are made from natural fibres. For painting large areas, a flat piece of stringybark roughly 15 cm long and up to 5 cm wide is used. Rubbing on the ground or chewing softens the end of the bark, separating the fibres and increasing its capacity to hold pigment. Fine brushes are made by inserting a piece of grass into a handle, or by carving a reed into a fine blade. The artist can chew the other end of the reed to make a medium-sized brush. Human hair can also be inserted into a handle to make fine brushes.

APPLICATION

Before the *rarrk* is painted, a background is applied to the painting surface. Traditionally, backgrounds were painted in red ochre, though multicoloured backgrounds are now widely used. A flat or monochrome background is created by applying the pigment evenly with the stringybark brushes. A textured background can be made by blowing the pigment from the mouth, or by using a manual spray gun. The artist can achieve different effects, depending on whether the surface is dry or wet before application. Figures and objects are kept within the boundaries of the painted surface.

While sitting with the bark or paper in his lap, the artist uses his brushes to create *rarrk*. The point of the brush is directed towards the artist and the pigment applied with smooth strokes away from the body. Layer upon layer of *rarrk* is painted, creating fine, detailed images. Frequently, artists depict internal structures and organs, thus the term 'X-ray' art is regularly used to define this unique painting style.

Applying rarrk or 'cross-hatching'

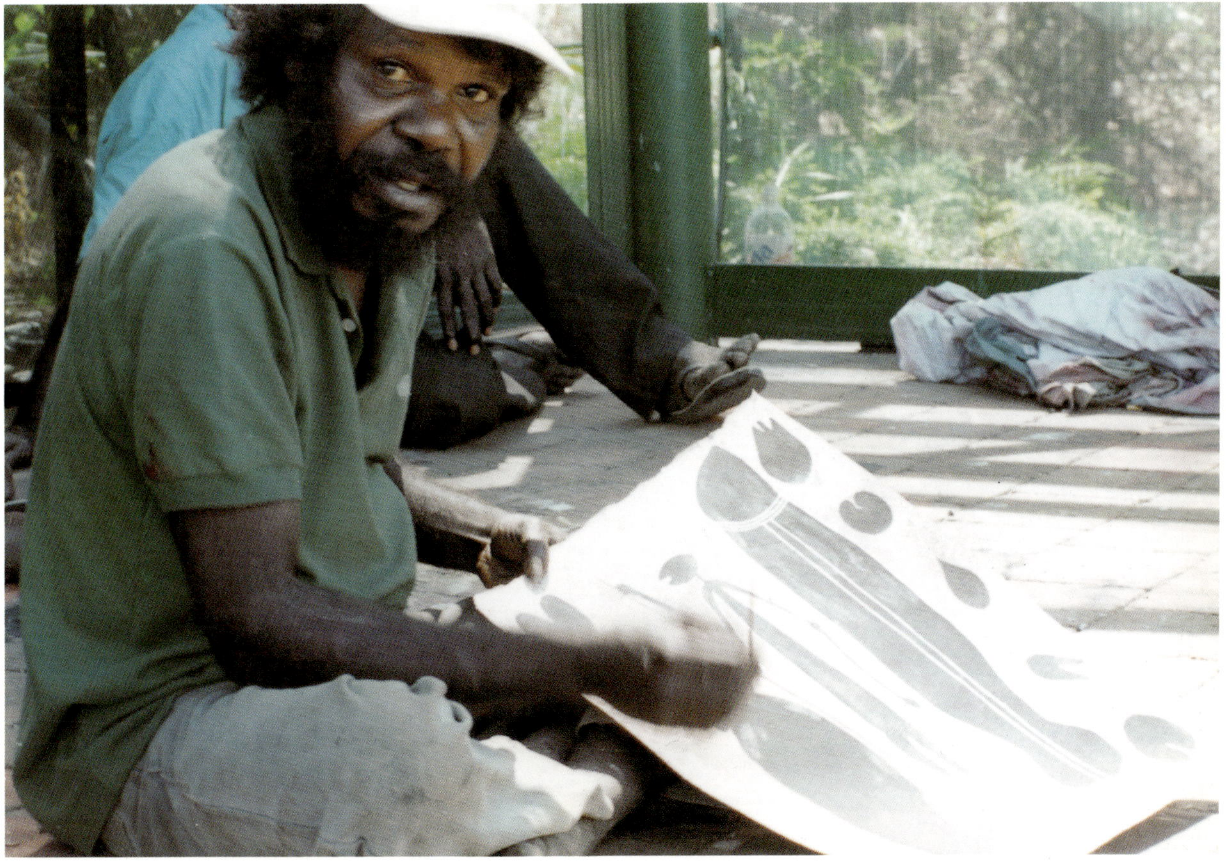

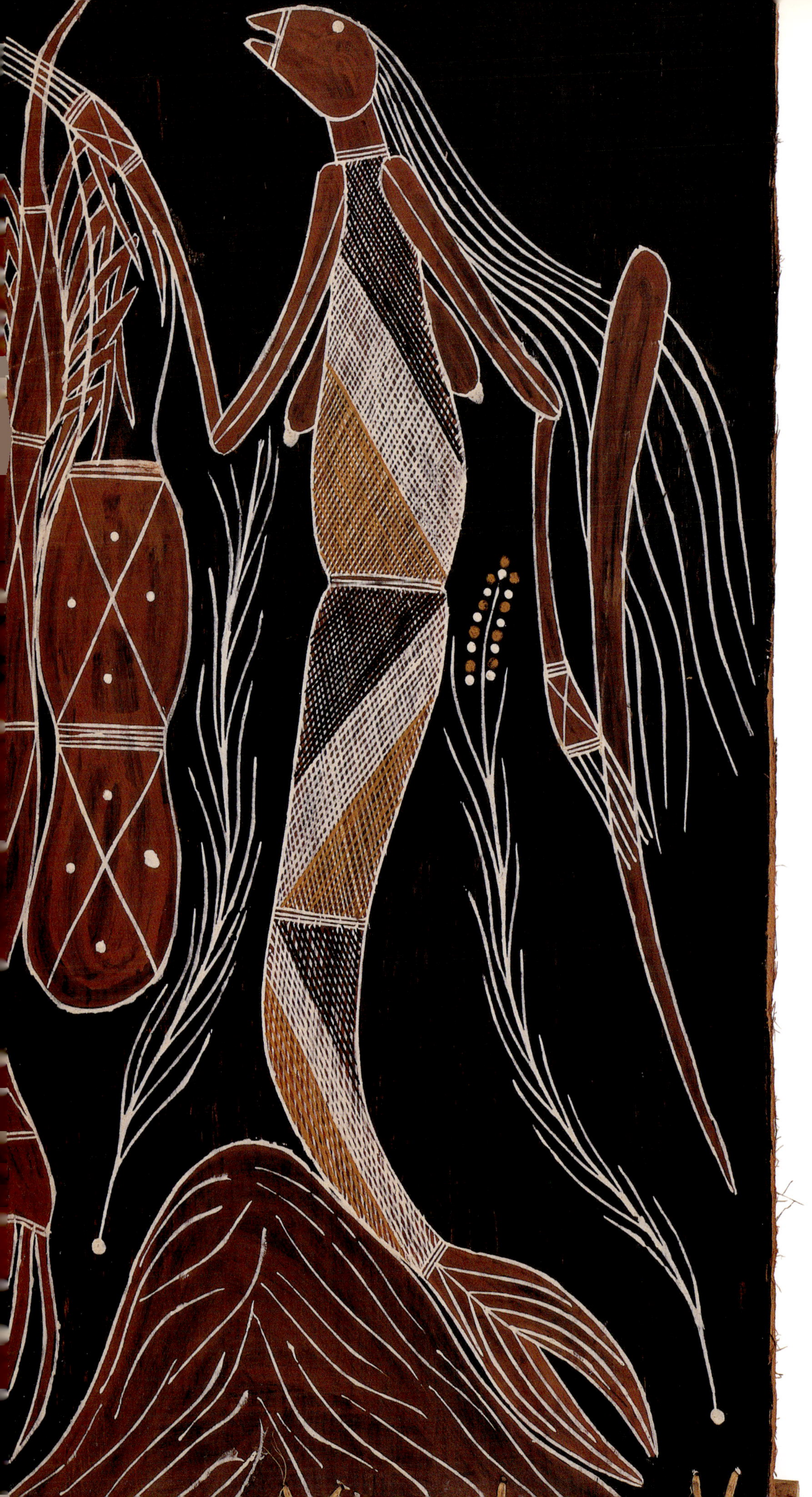

S.H.

Like rock, bark is a traditional painting surface. With increasing European contact and the advent of a market for local art, the use of bark has increased significantly. Barks are collected seasonally from December through to April-May. Sheets of bark are easier to collect and prepare during the Wet, as the bark of the stringybark tree (*Eucalyptus tetrodonta*) is softer and easier to cut. It is also more pliable. During the Dry, bark is inclined to split.

To obtain a sheet of bark the tree is cut around its circumference. Two rings are made a short distance apart. A single straight cut along the length then joins these rings. The bark is peeled off and the tree is effectively ringbarked. When removed, the bark maintains its circular (hollow) shape.

To flatten the bark, a fire is made and allowed to burn down to hot coals. The wet bark is placed on the fire and pressed flat, with the outside of the bark in contact with the coals. The surface to be painted does not come

Painting on Bark

into contact with the fire, thus preventing it from being blackened or burnt. Once flat, the bark is laid on the ground for a few days until dry, held flat by sticks, stones or other objects. A straight stick is then tied along each end to ensure its flatness. It is then ready to be decorated.

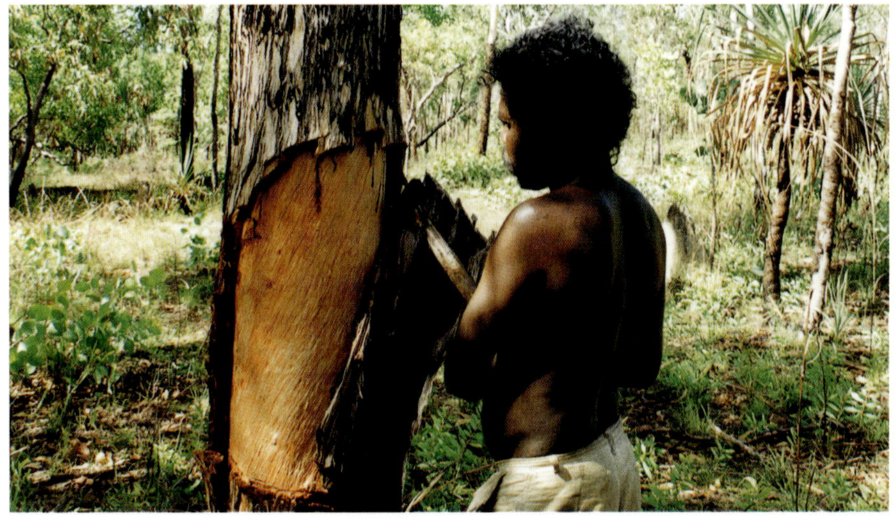

LEFT: *Using an axe, bark is peeled from the stringy bark tree*

OPPOSITE: Yawk Yawk Spirit Sunbathing, *by Abraham Dakgalawuy, private collection*

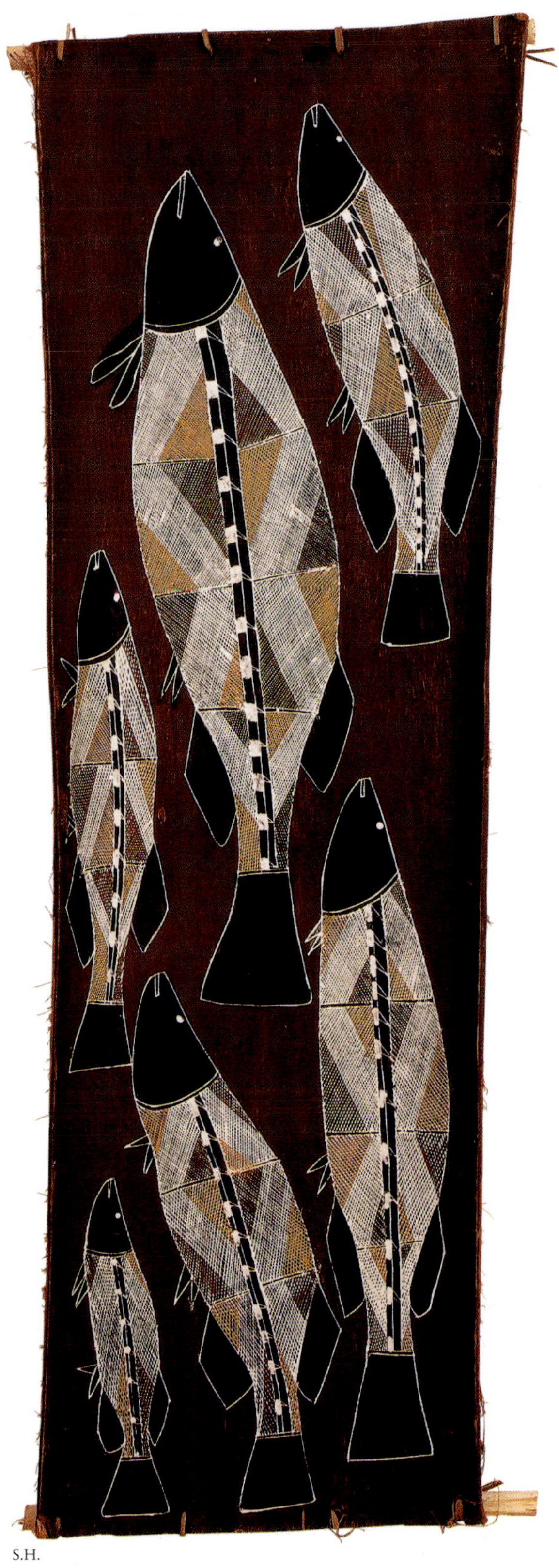

S.H.

School of Saratoga, *by Joshua Bangar, private collection*

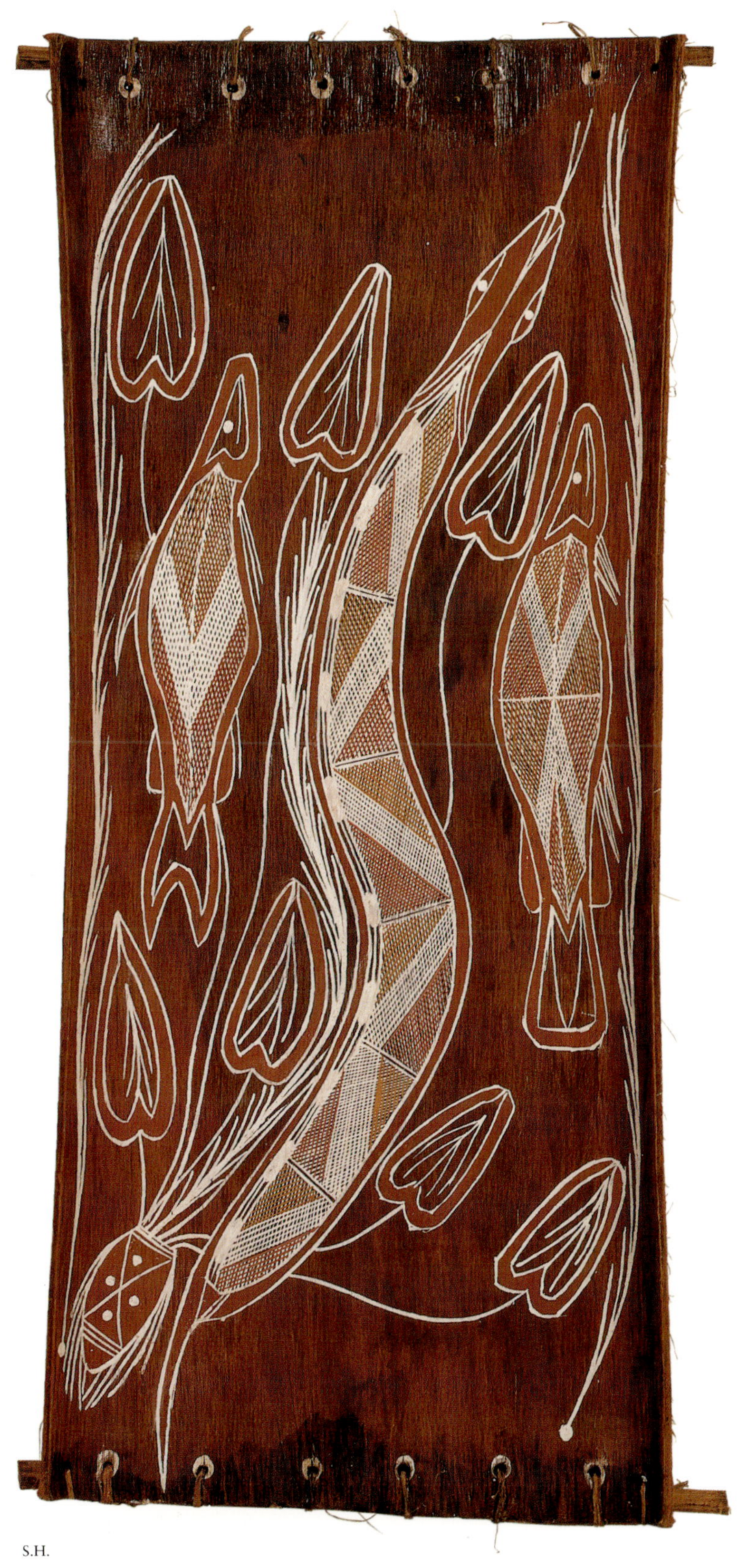

Swimming Serpent, *by Abraham Dakgalawuy, private collection*

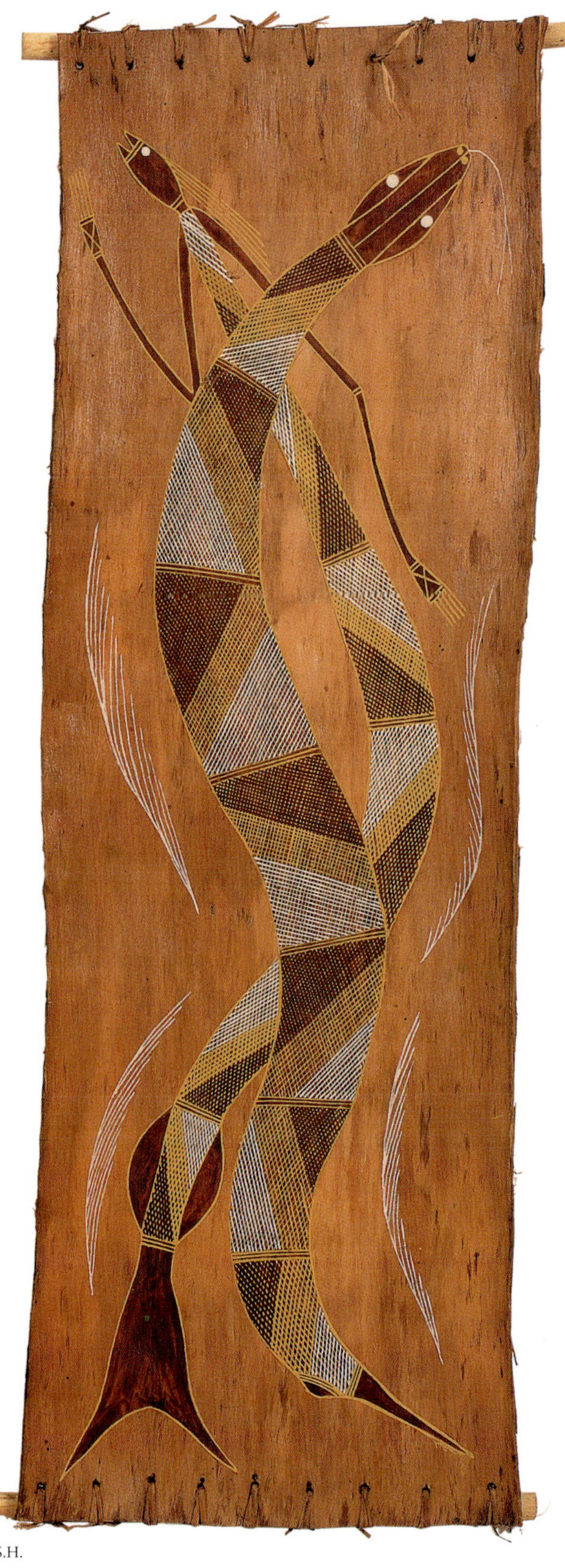

Rainbow Serpent and Mermaid, *by Mark Nadjongorle, private collection*

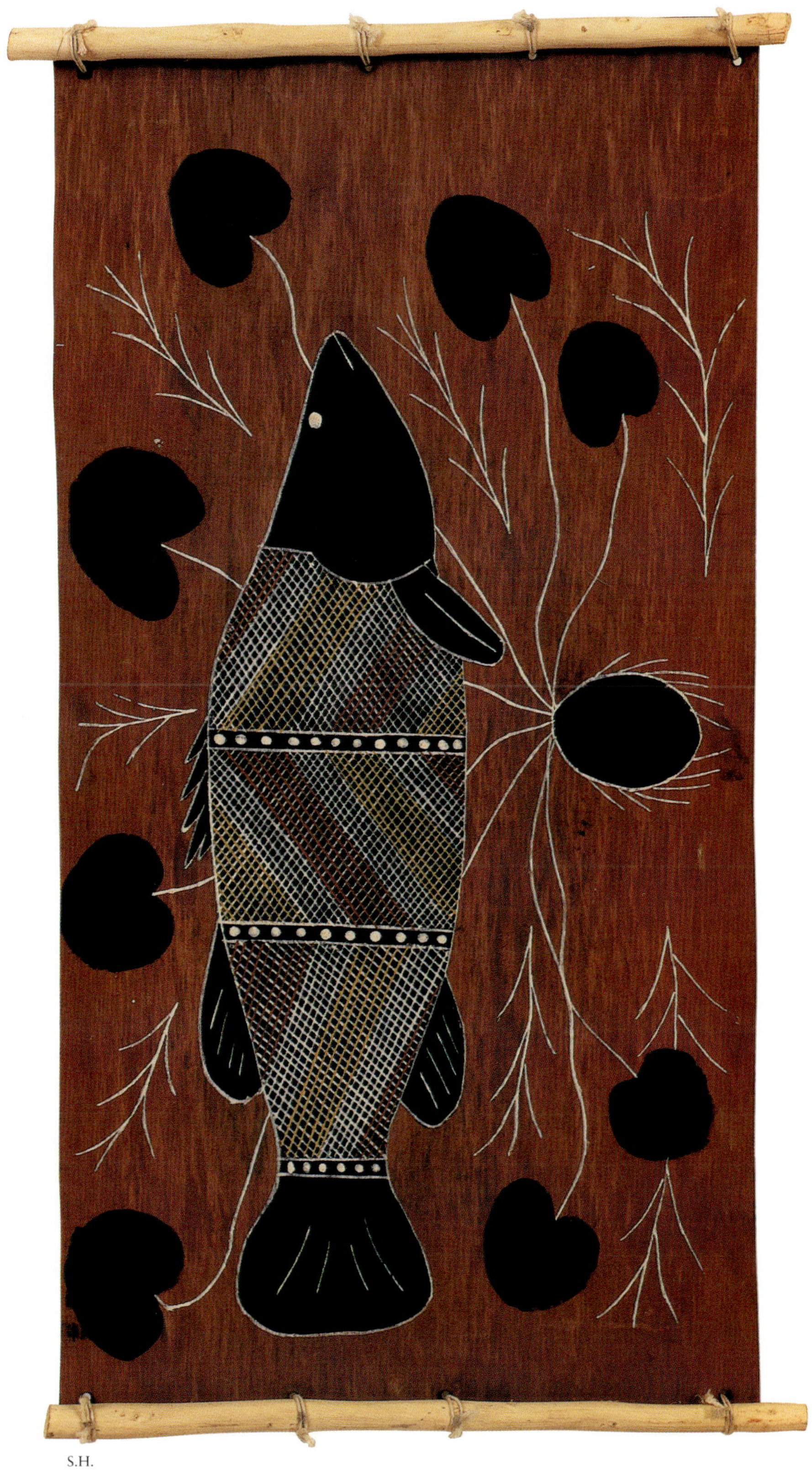

Barramundi, *by John Lemibanda, private collection*

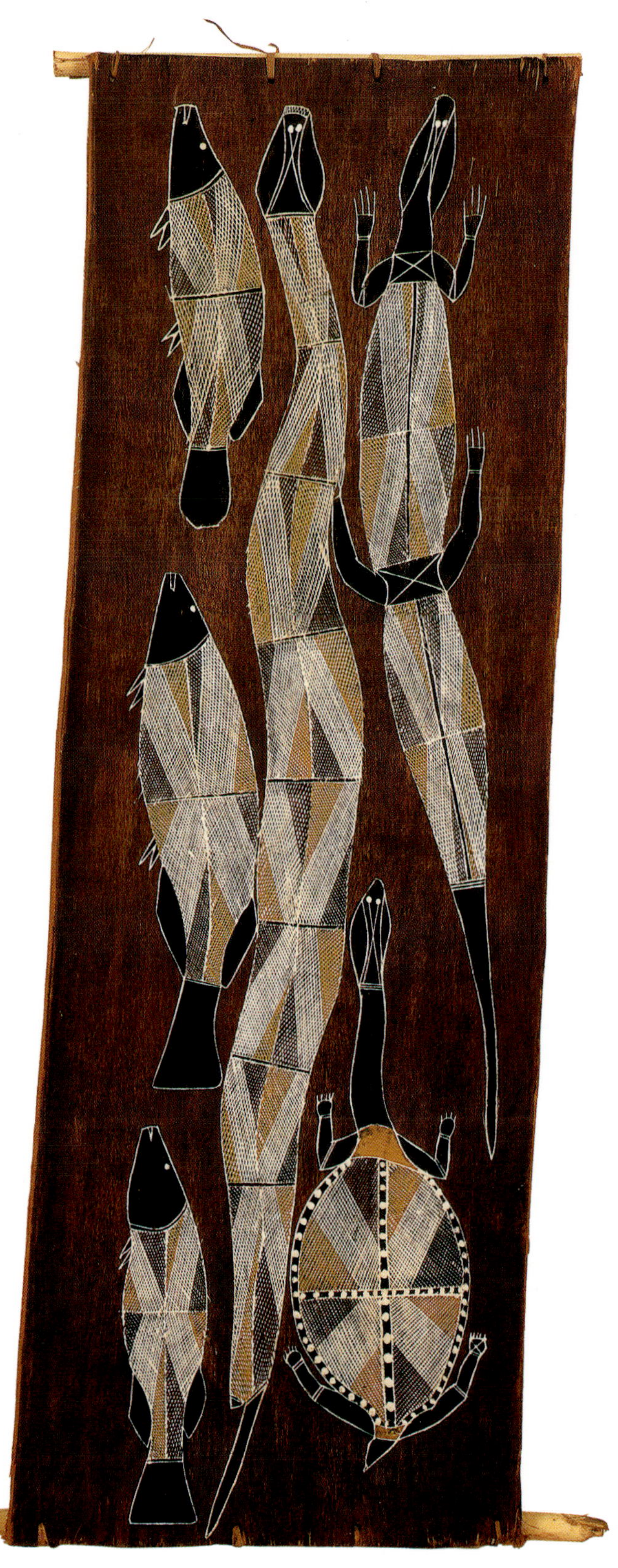

S.H.

Goanna, Turtle, Snake and Saratoga, *by Joshua Bangar, private collection*

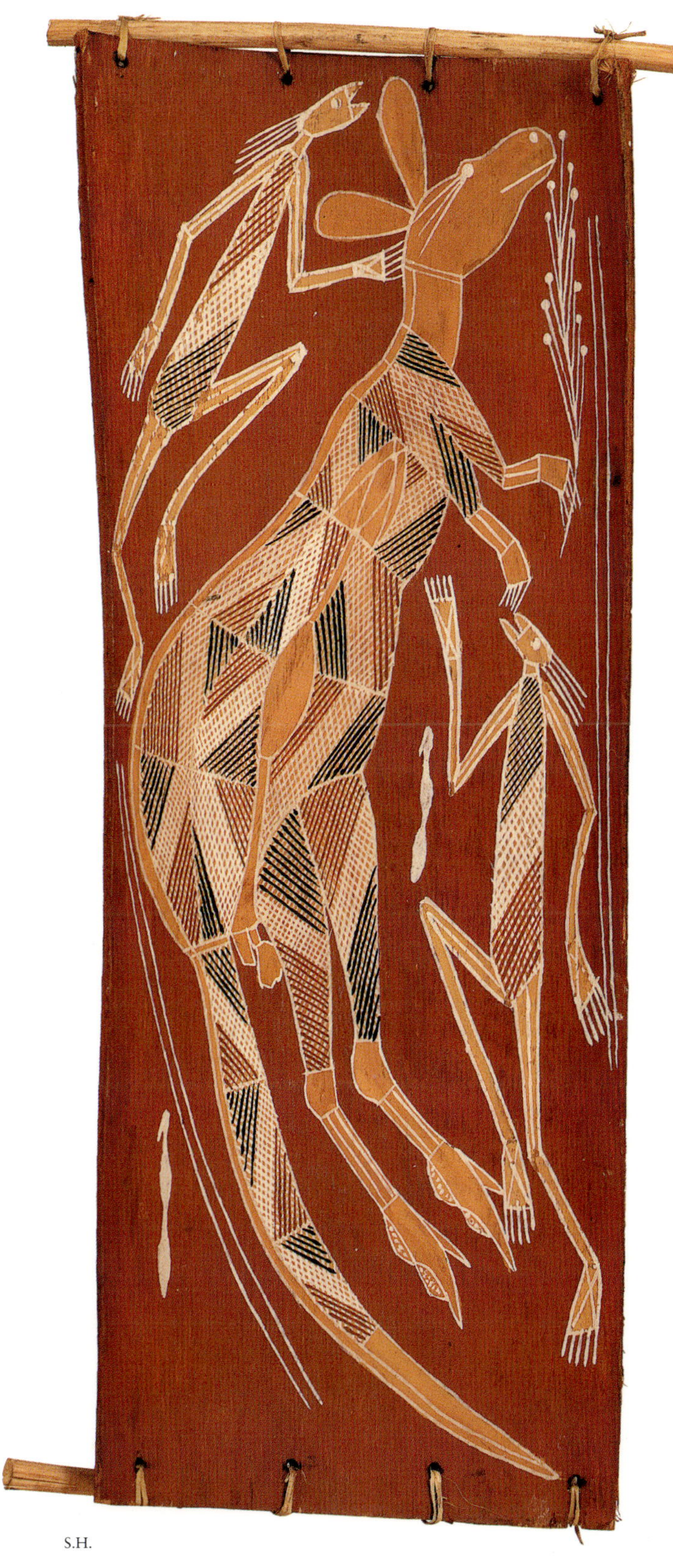

Mimi Men Hunting Kangaroo, *by Mark Nadjongorle, private collection*

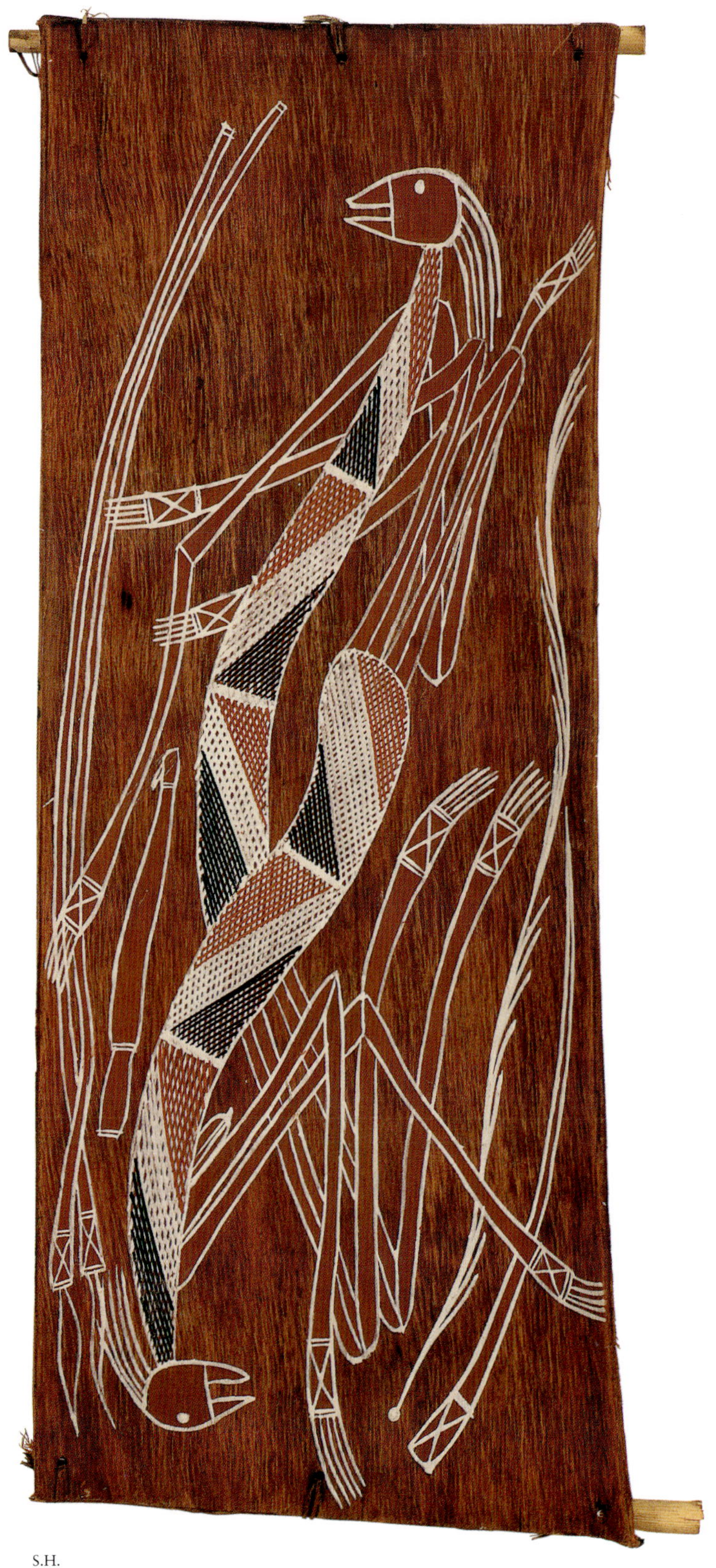

Mimi Men Hunting, *by Abraham Dakgalawuy, private collection*

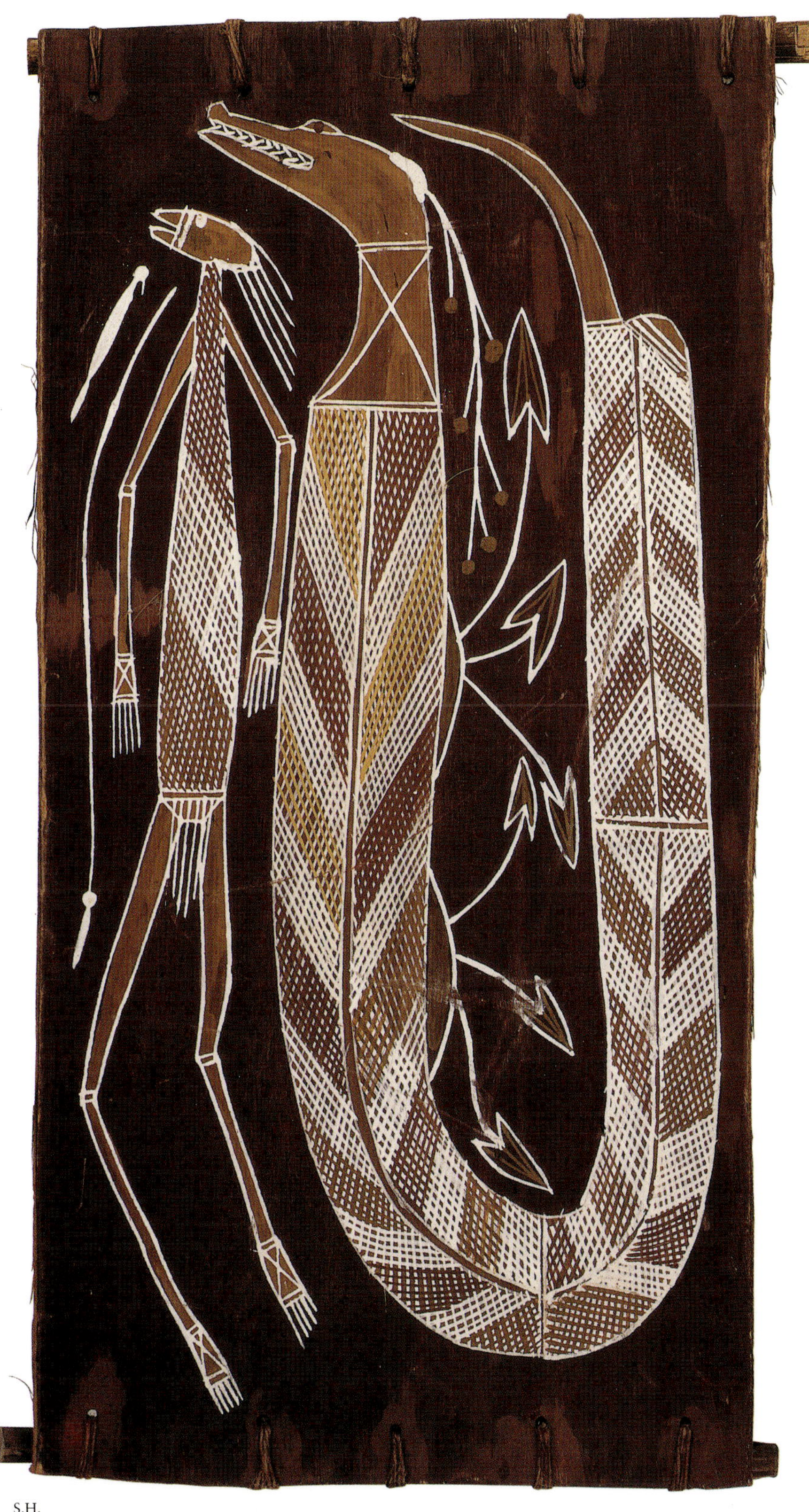

Ngalkunburriyaymi, the Rainbow Serpent, *by Abraham Dakgalawuy, private collection*

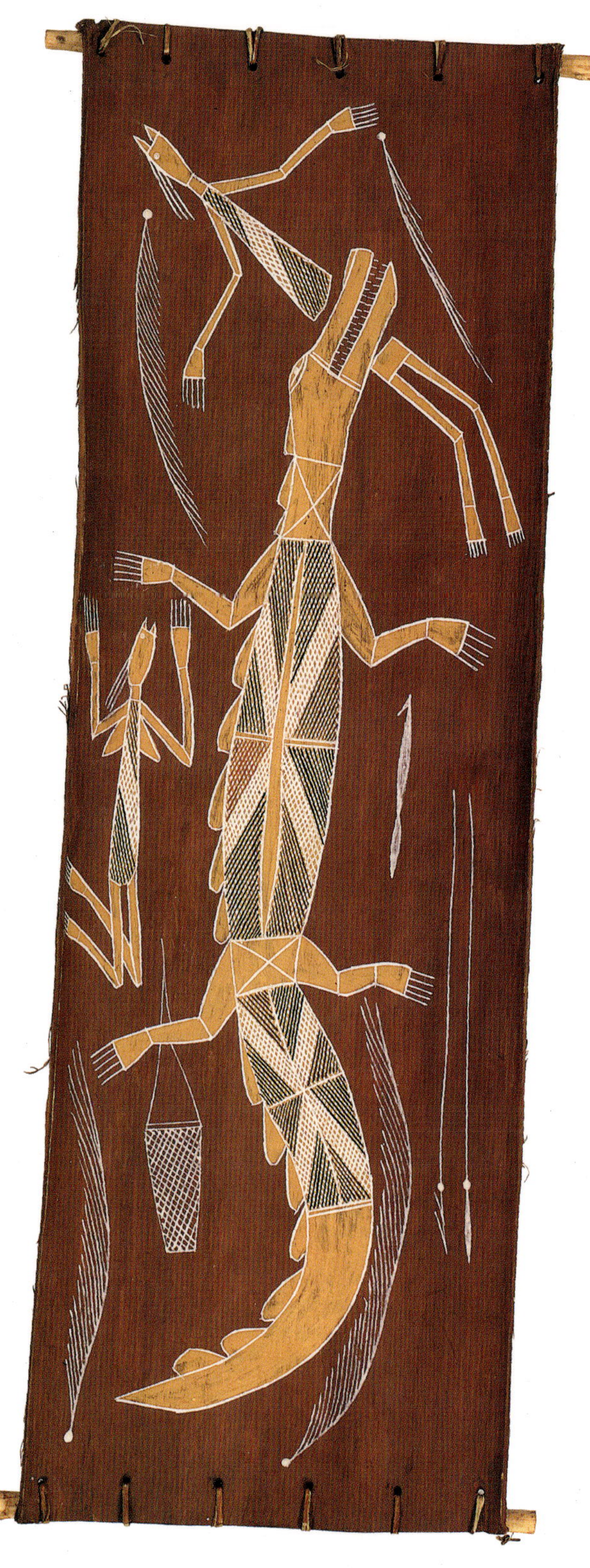

S.H.

Man Being Eaten by Crocodile, by Chris Ngaboy, private collection

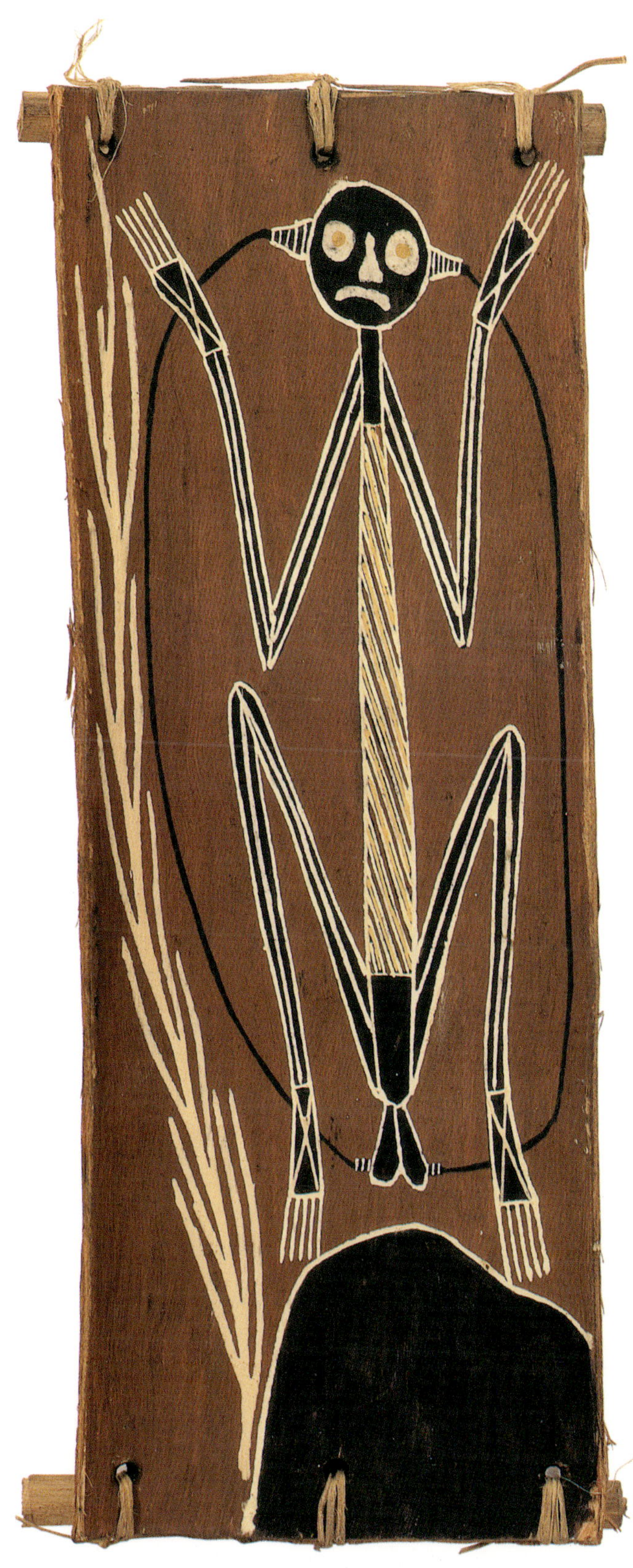

Namarrkon (Lightning Man), by David Cameron, private collection

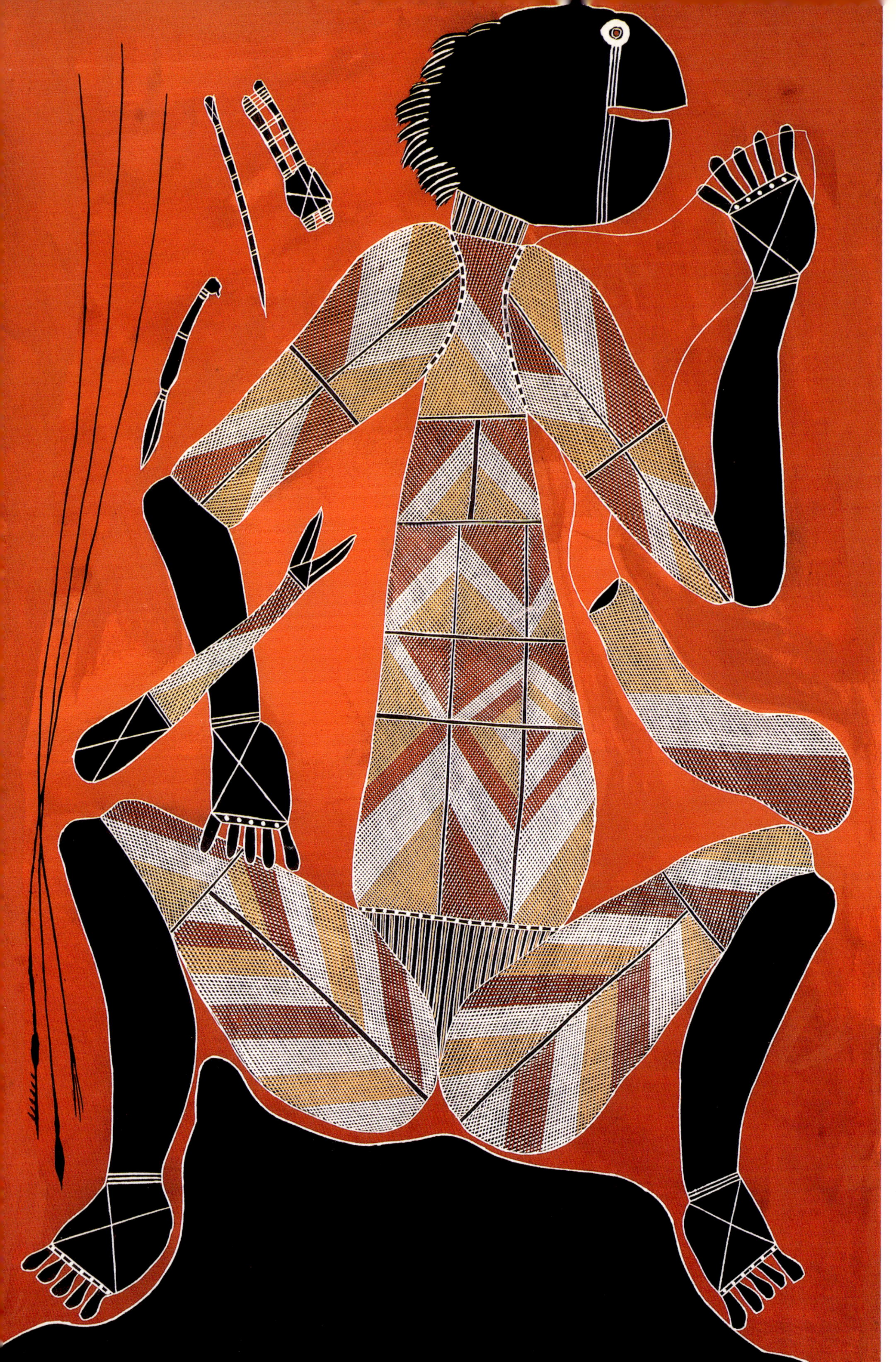

S.H.

In recent years, many artists have begun to paint on paper in addition to traditional painting surfaces. Thick cotton rag paper is mostly used. It has several features that make it appealing. Firstly is its availability, as it becomes harder to obtain bark towards the end of the Dry. Secondly, paper is more durable and less inclined to perish or warp after many years. Thirdly, it can be framed. The techniques of ochre application for works on paper are the same as have been practised for thousands of years on other surfaces.

Luma come from sea from up north after being born from Yingarna. He was born as a man, so he came [to Marlwon, Alex's country] and saw two sisters, two sisters, and he was walking, going with them two ladies. So Luma he made babies with the two ladies. Their names were Marrayka and Likanaya. He also made babies with Ngalkunburriyaymi, another lady. Marrayka and Ngalkunburriyaymi were two sister. Their spirits stay now at Marlwon, that's

Works on Paper

my Dreaming. Marrayka and Likanaya. Ngalkunburriyaymi she left. Luma had been travelling all around, walking, looking around the place.

Yingarna said to Luma: go and get these two ladies and you make them so they will make, you know, barramundi fish Dreaming. She gave him stories told him to go, Yingarna said to him. So Yingarna stays at the sea, he came out in the fresh water so he found the two ladies and they made babies. That when they made fish the barramundi Dreaming. He makes all the fresh water fish and creeks, billabongs, turtles, all that, file snakes, he made brim and all that [djang].

After making babies Luma just went, he travelled around, north, east, west, he came from north so he just travelled around, west, east, south. The girls turned into mermaids, they live in the water. They turn into mermaids after he's left.

With Luma [in the painting] are a dilly bag, stone axe, sticks for digging, bondock [woomera] and mearu [fighting stick], three spears, a fighting spear, shovel spear and fishing spear.

Luma Luma the Giant, *by Alex Nganjmirra, 66 x 101 cm*

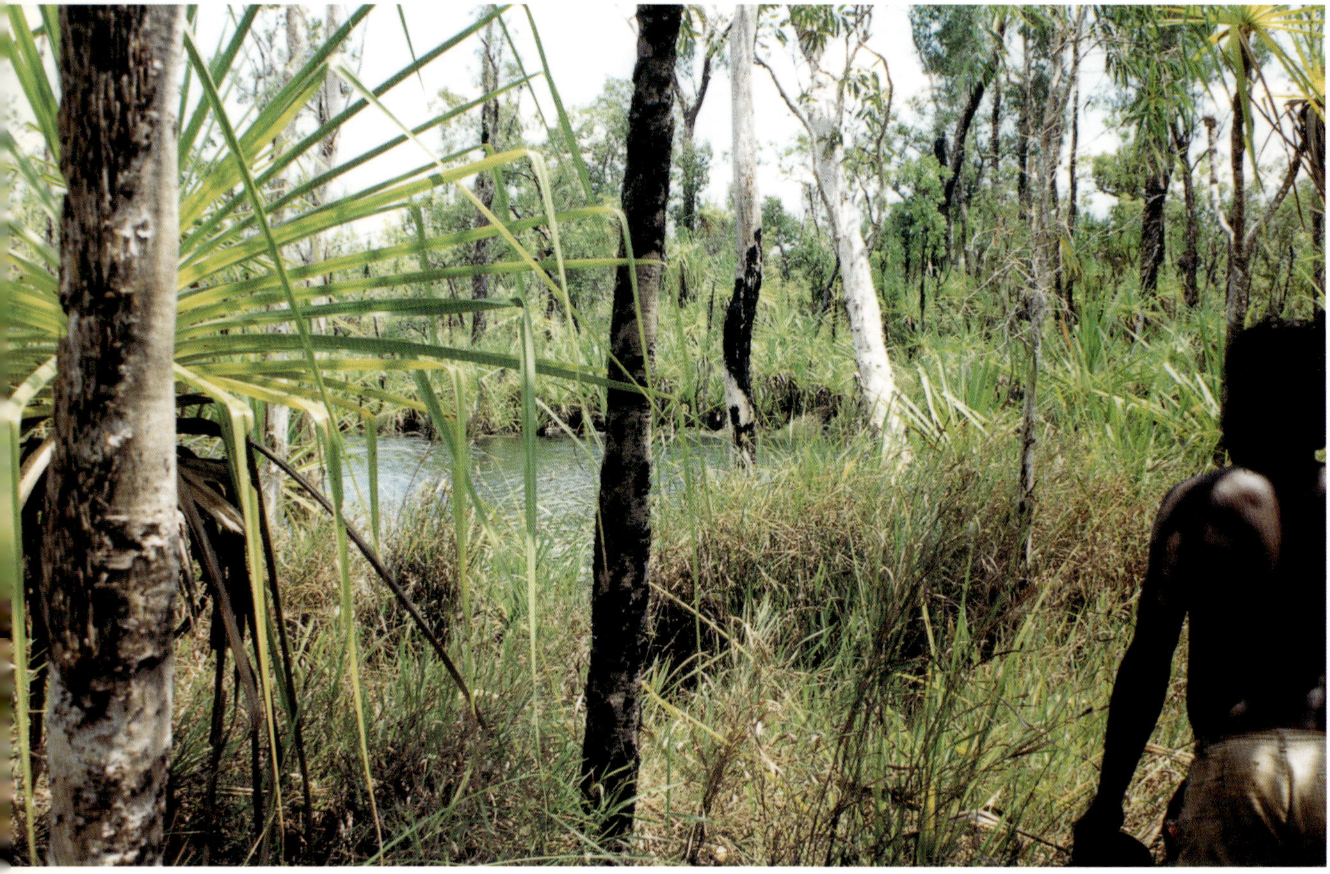

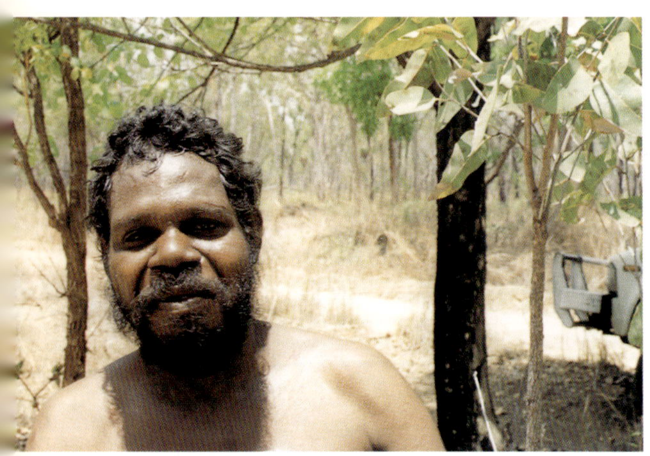

This one is not my Dreaming. The man's name is Bluey, that's his Dreaming. He said to me I can paint it. Bluey paints my Dreaming so I paint his. My Dreaming is Yawk Yawk [freshwater mermaids]. His is Luma, so Bluey can paint Yawk Yawk, my Dreaming, and I paint Luma.

You can see the rarrk, the crosshatching, that is mine, Yirridja. Bluey is Dhuwa. The red, yellow, white and black we both share that one with Dhuwa, both share. We have a ceremony, Kunapipi, all that, we paint our bodies and start work, dancing, them colours. White, red, yellow and black.

Luma carries the dilly bags, the ones for feathers, for ceremony. Mardayin and Lorrcon ceremony. He also carries other objects for ceremony, and colours. Luma's spirit is in the pool at Marlwon with Marrayka and Likanaya. That's my djang, Yawk Yawk.

Alex Nganjmirra

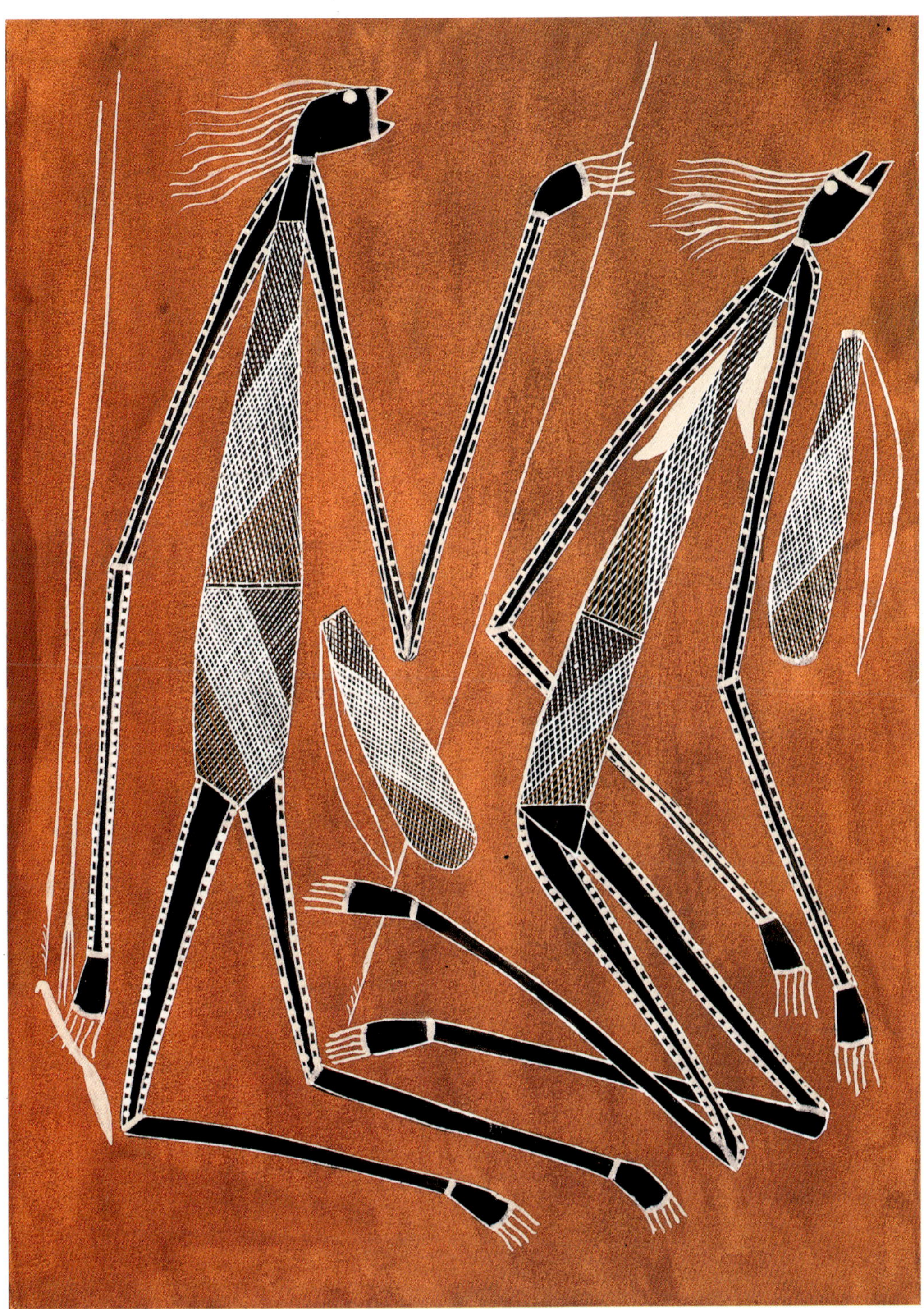

S.H.

Mimi Spirits, *by Thompson Nganjmirra, 51 x 72 cm*

Mimi spirits, nonphysical beings who have been present and active since Creation, are credited with having taught Kunwinjku people to hunt. This painting depicts a male *Mimi* carrying hunting and fishing spears and a spear thrower. A female *Mimi* carries dilly bags used for holding food and sundry items.

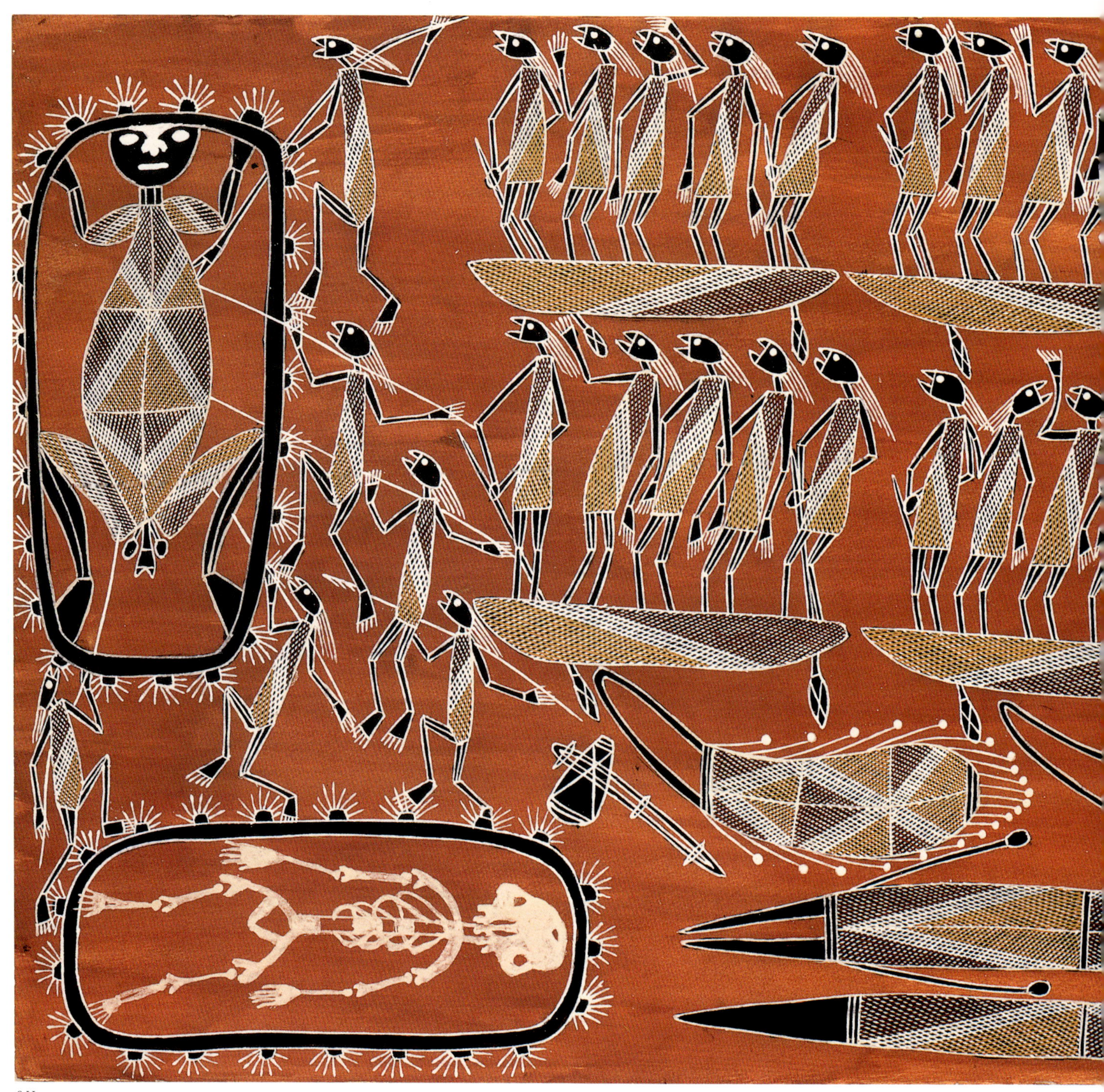

The Killing of Luma Luma, *by Danny Djorlom, 101 x 66 cm*

Luma Luma the giant taught the Kunwinjku people the sacred knowledge of the Mardayin ceremony. His dilly bags contain the *rangga* (sacred objects) for the ceremony. Luma, however, did not teach the Kunwinjku all the sacred information, instead he used his knowledge to his benefit, demanding favours, especially women, in return for the knowledge. Angered at Luma's constant taking of their women, *Binninj* men of both skin groups joined forces to kill Luma. They

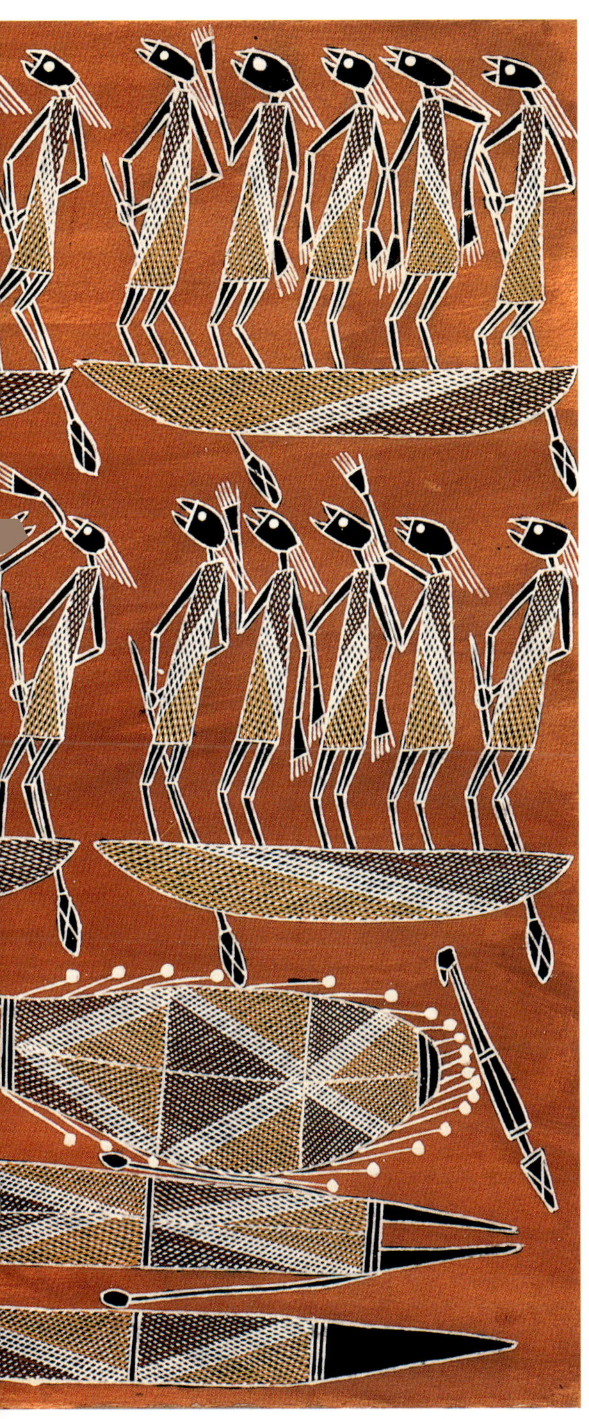

chased him in their boats and speared him while he slept under a tree. In this painting the *Binninj* people can be seen spearing Luma while he sleeps. His dead body lies in the foreground. The dilly bags contain the sacred ceremonial objects captured from him. One contains objects to be used by the *Dhuwa*, while the other contains objects for *Yirridja*. Ceremonial dancing sticks lie below the dilly bags. The songs, dances and ceremonial objects are different for each skin group.

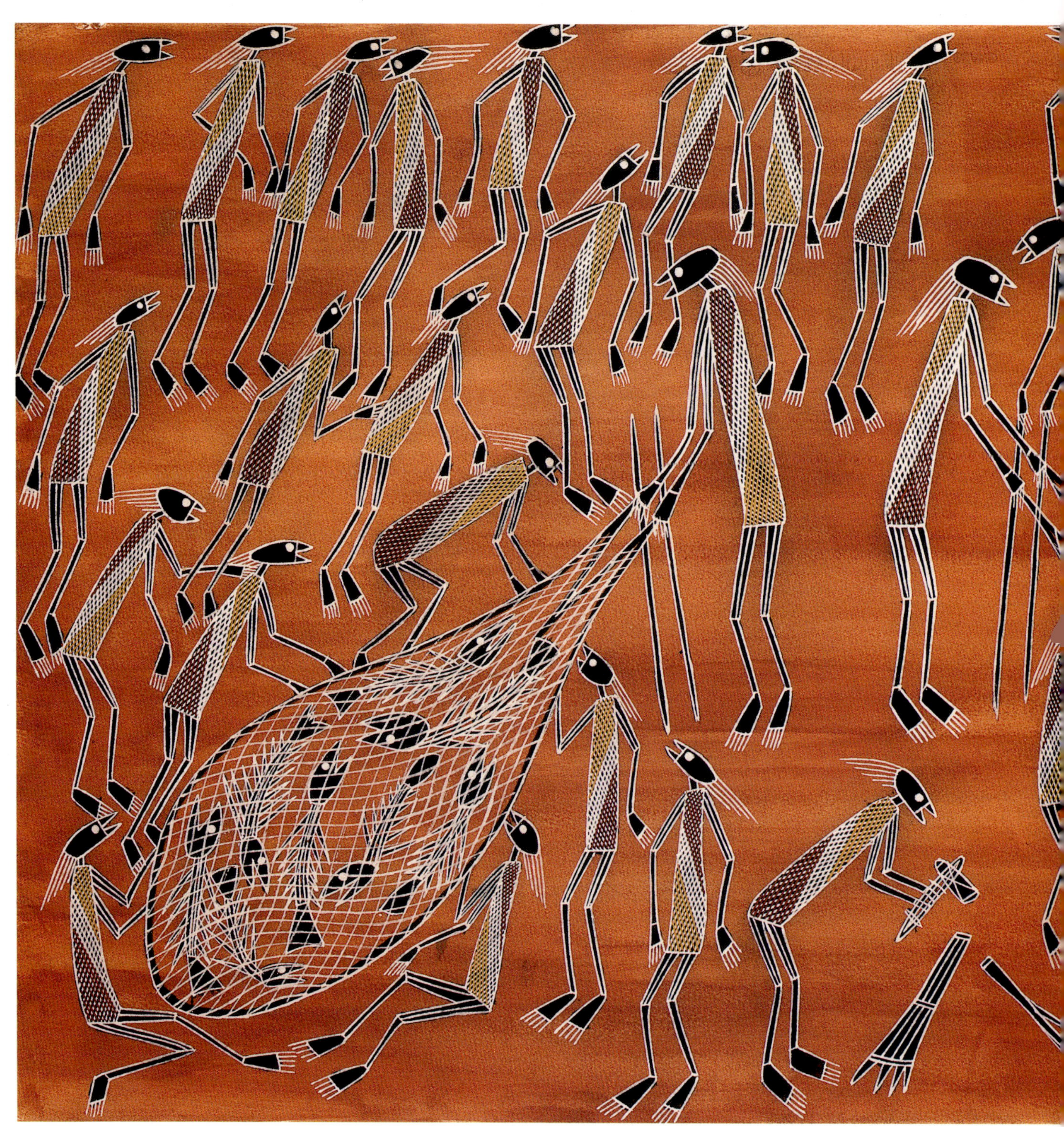

S.H.

Crow Dreaming, *by Danny Djorlom, 101 x 66 cm*

This is an old time story ... for two to three days he couldn't get any fish because he was too late
so he got angry and cut one special tree, dreaming there to make big storm come, and floods. So
he went and cut the tree and made big storm. This made a creek, cut it in half made it into two

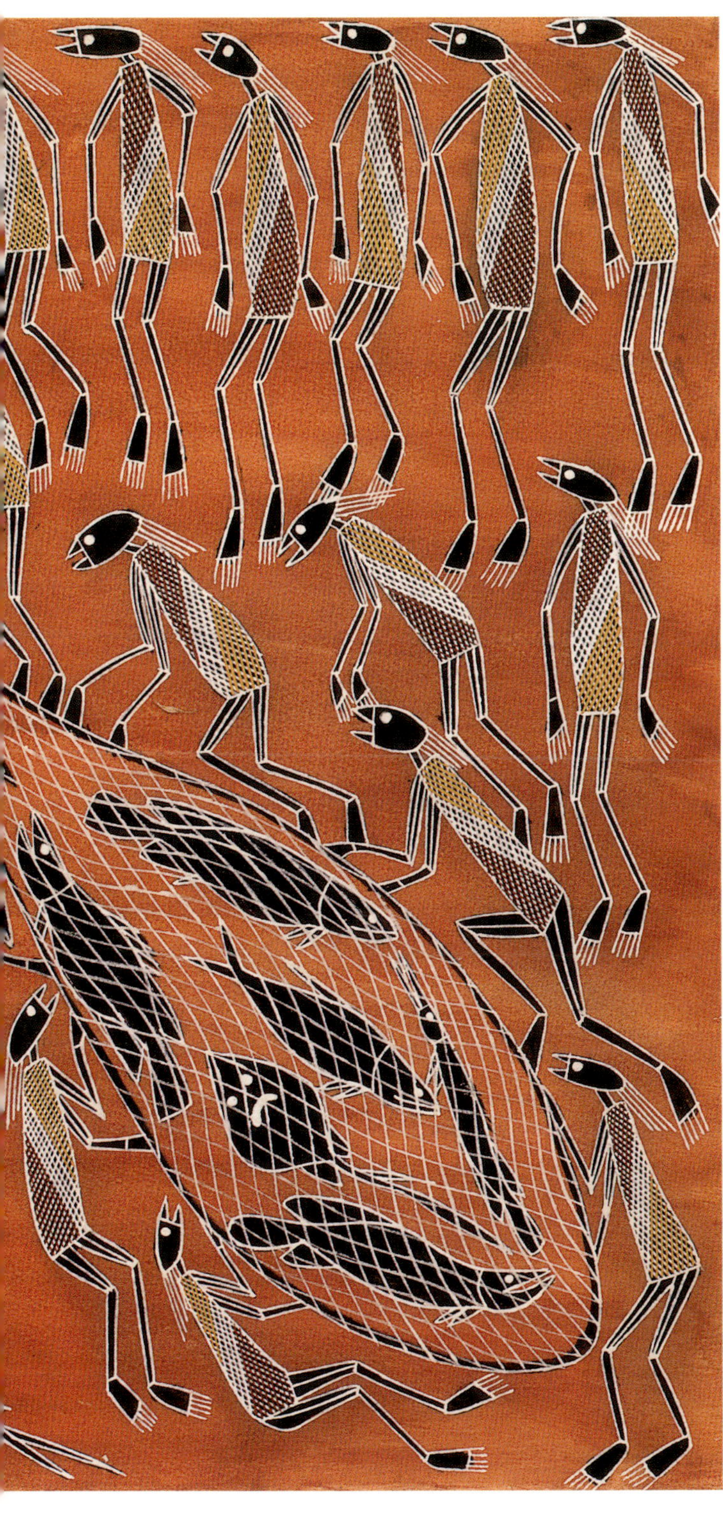

The central figures are the crow people and the pelican people, the peoples of north and south Goulburn Island, which during the Dreamtime formed a single island. The crow people were checking their fishing nets too late in the morning. The pelican people had raided them and only scraps were left.The net on the left contains the fish that the early birds (pelican people) have eaten. The fish in the right net are the fish the early birds are taking home to their families. On the left are the crow people who have been left only scraps. On the right are the pelican people. The crows are *Dhuwa* and the pelicans are *Yirridja*.

BELOW: *Artist Danny Djorlom*

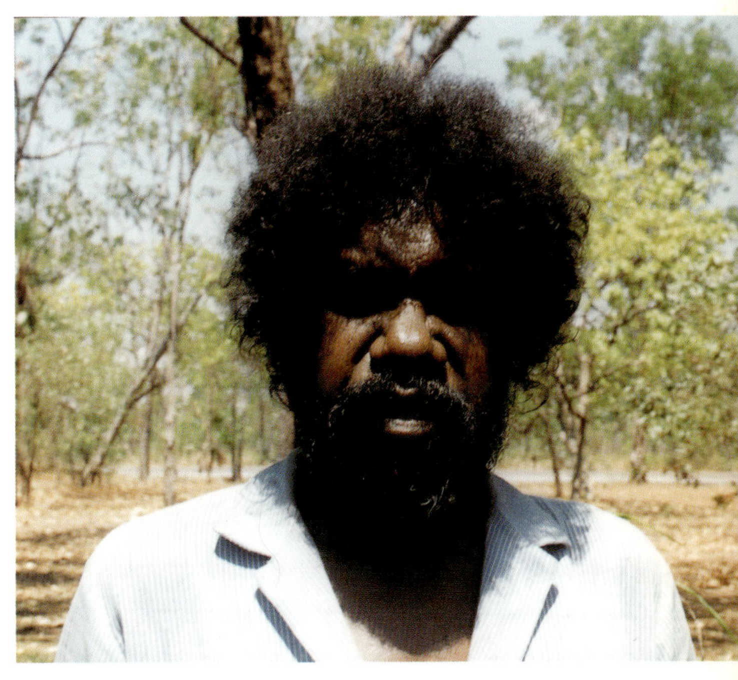

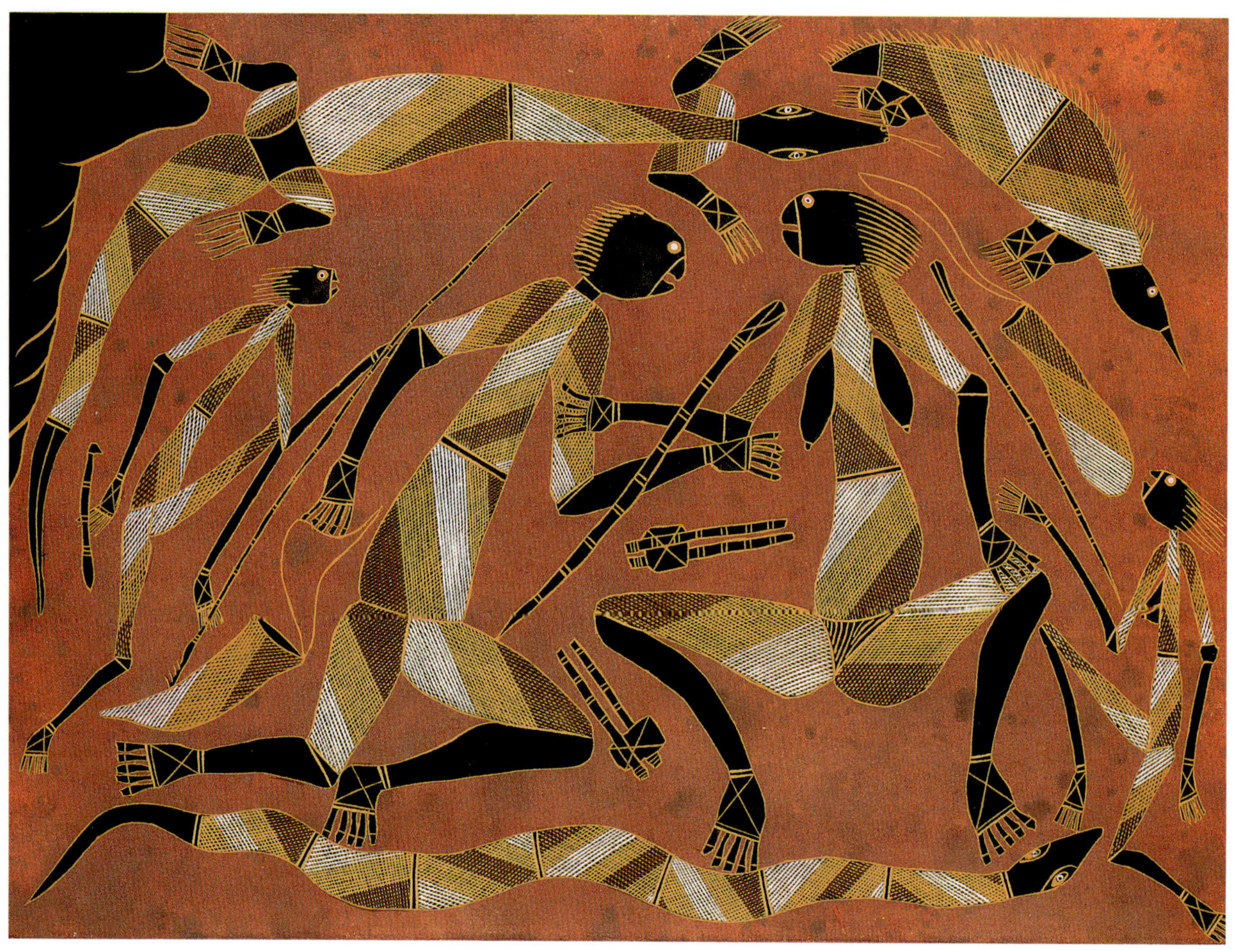

S.H.

Luma and Marrayka, *by Alex Nganjmirra, 77 x 56 cm*

This painting depicts Luma and Marrayka initiating their courtship. A goanna, echidna, snake and two *Mimi* surround them. A hunting spear and spear thrower, digging sticks, dilly bags and stone axes are also present.

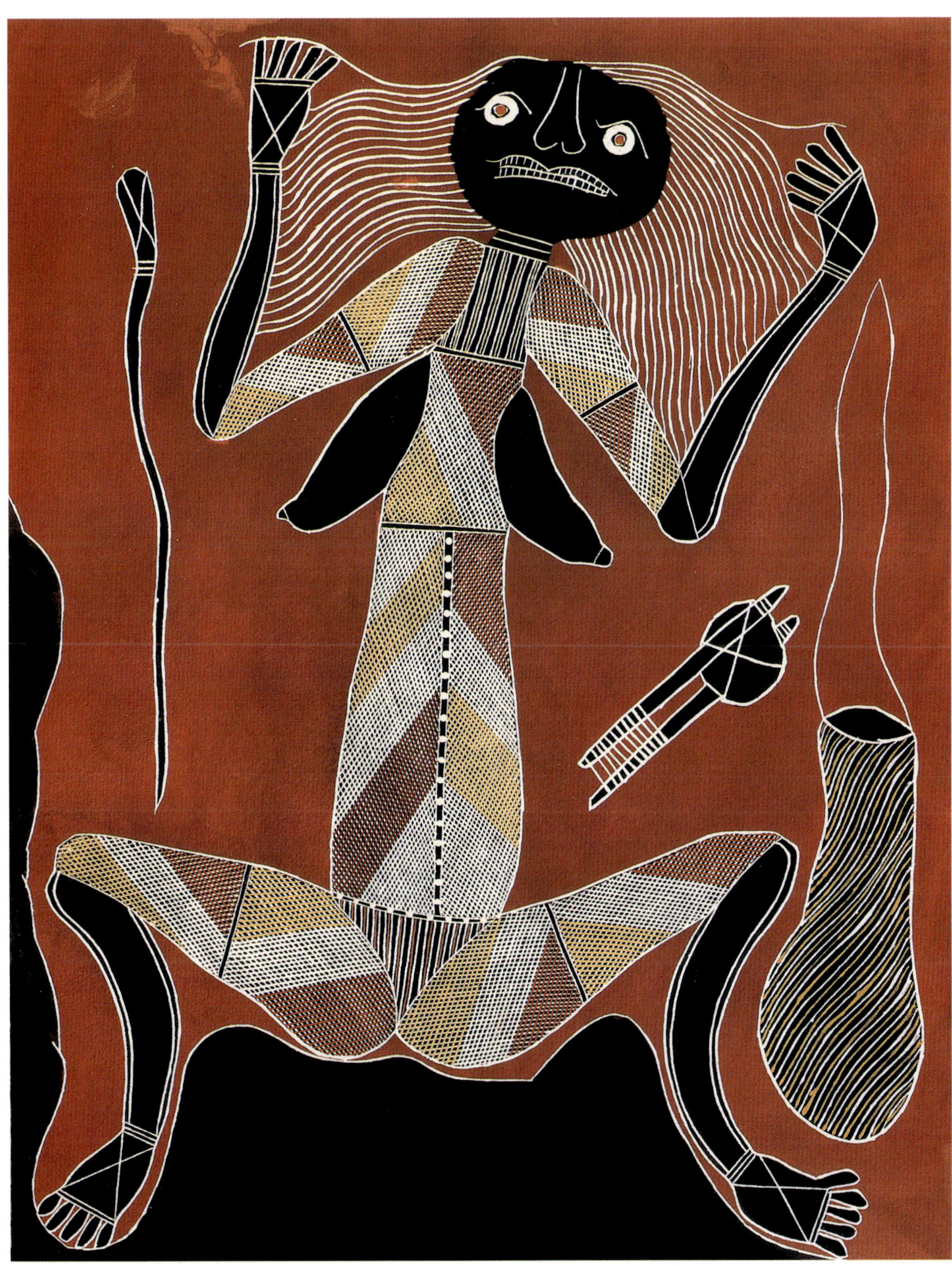

Marrayka, *by Alex Nganjmirra, 51 x 66 cm*

Here Marrayka, the younger of the Marlwon Dreaming sisters, from whom the Nganjmirras are descended, can be seen beautifying herself for the attention of Luma. She is running her fingers through her hair while a dilly bag, stone axe and digging stick lie beside her.

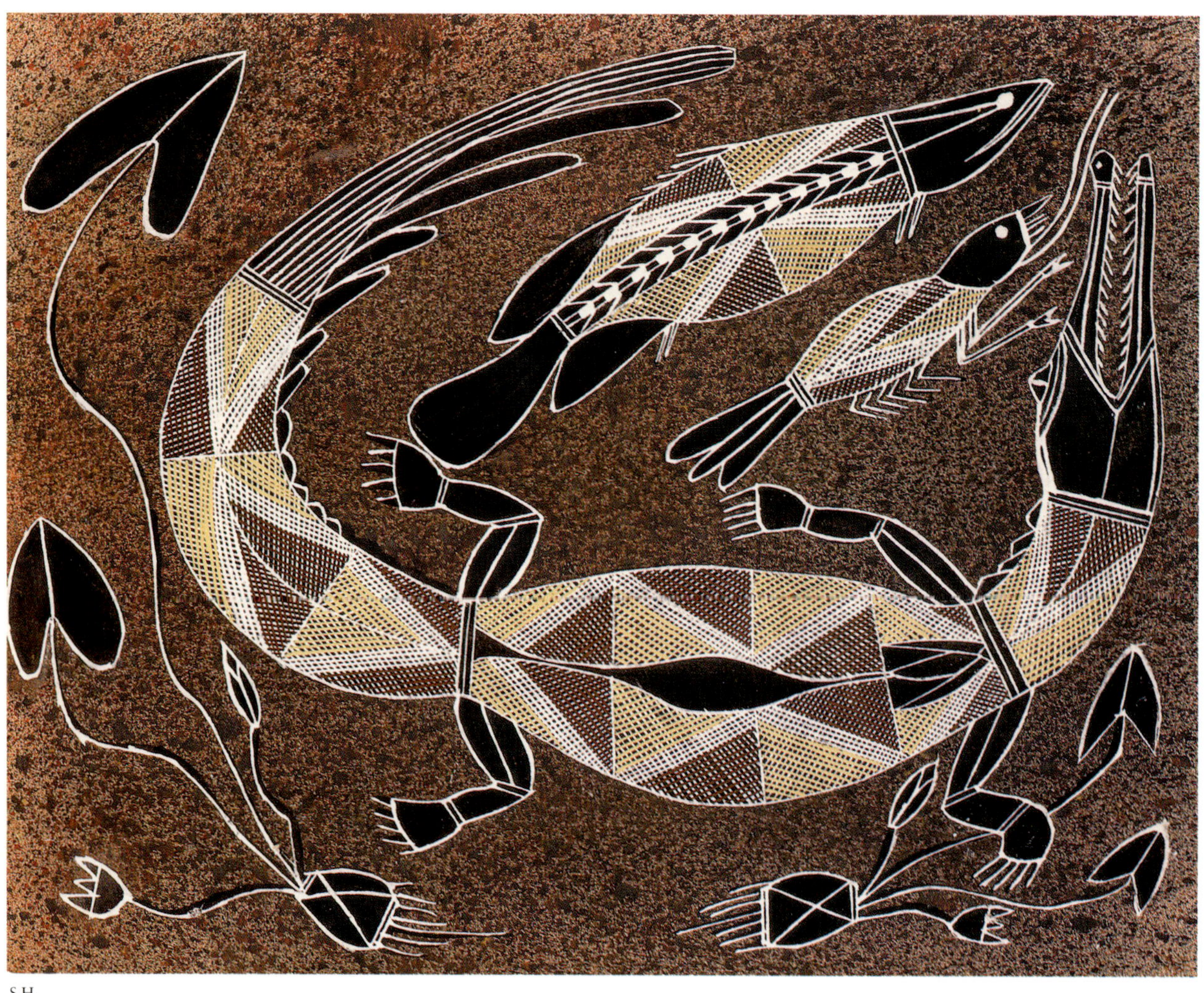

S.H.

Crocodile, Barramundi and Shrimp, *by Danny Djorlom, 66 x 51 cm*

The freshwater crocodile is *djang* (sacred) for the *Dhuwa* skin group, as are most marine animals

such as barramundi and shrimp.

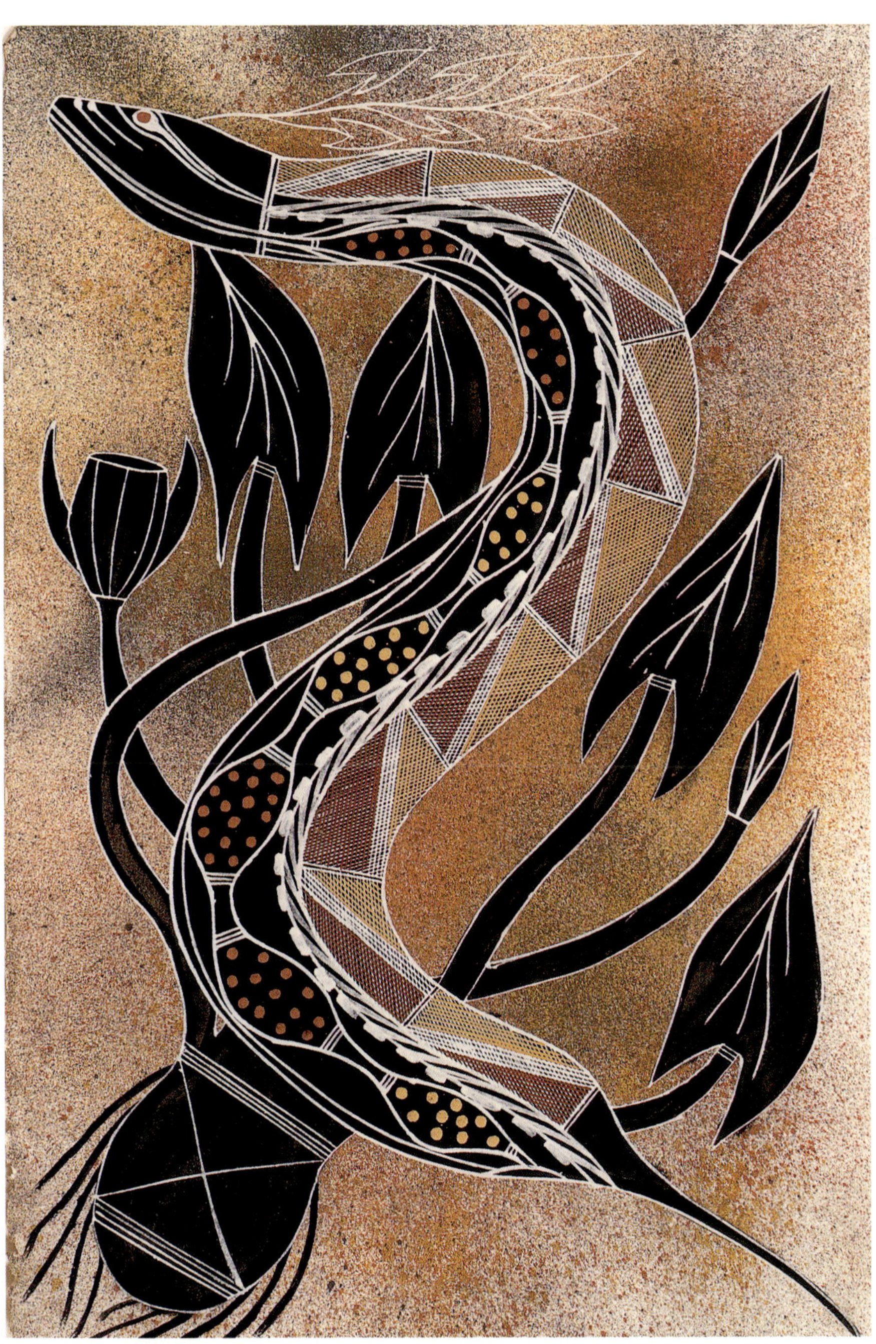

The Rainbow Serpent, *by Abraham Dakgalawuy, 51 x 76 cm*

The Rainbow Serpent, *Ngalyod*, is the most powerful Creation being, born of his mother, *Yingarna*. Mythology relating to the Rainbow Serpent transcends tribal and racial boundaries throughout much of Aboriginal Australia. *Ngalyod* created many features of the landscape, including waterways, billabongs and rivers. It is in these that he generally resides. He might also be seen in the sky during the Wet, when the process of renewal begins. *Ngalyod* regurgitates the water (rain) and animals he has swallowed during the Dry season. This process of swallowing and regurgitation is the central theme of the Kunapipi ceremony.

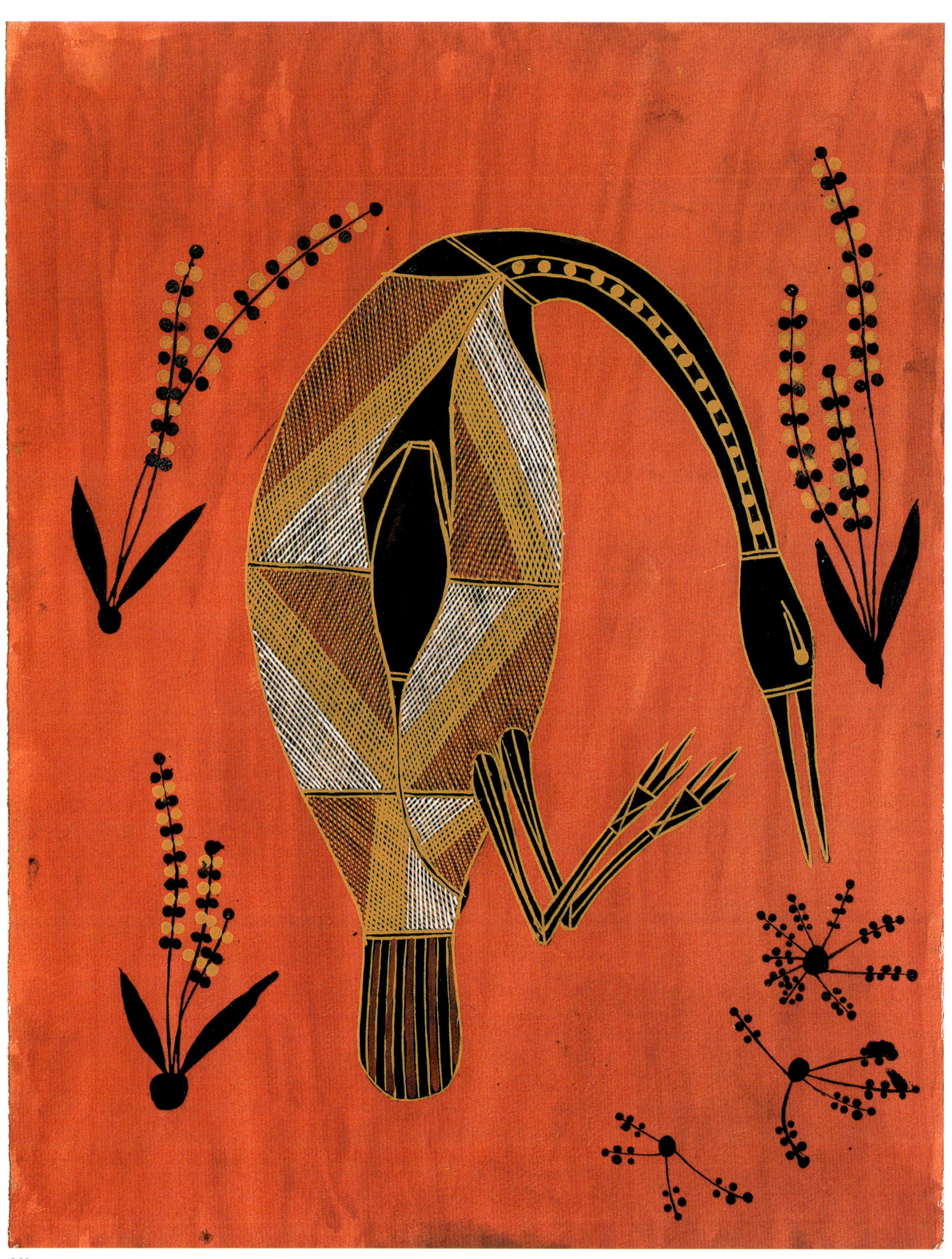

S.H.

Brolga, *by Mark Nadjongorle, 51 x 66 cm*

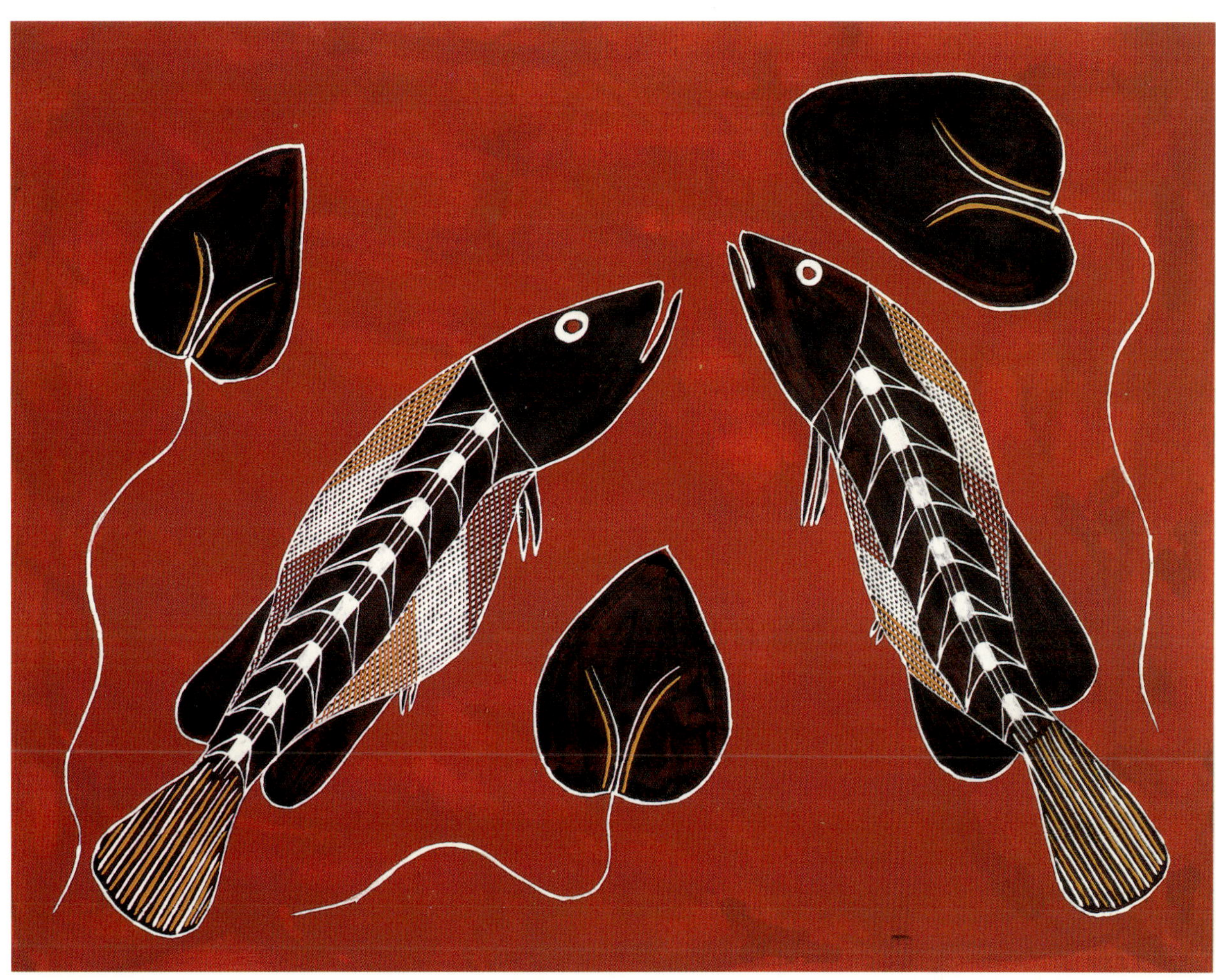

Barramundi, *by Alex Nganjmirra, 66 x 50 cm*

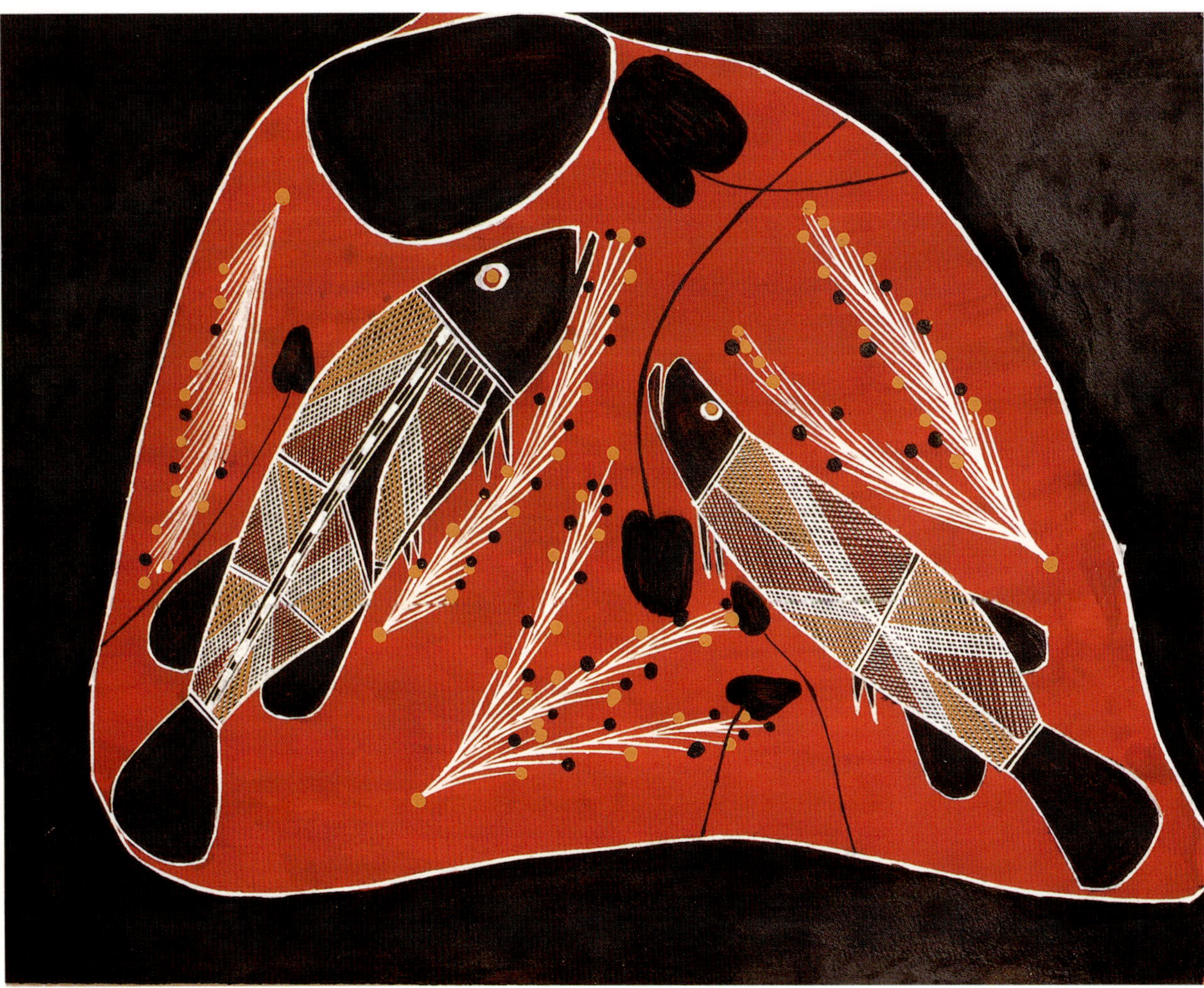

Trapped Fish, *by John Lemibanda, 60 x 51 cm*

After the Wet season has passed, and the Dry is well established, many flowing waterways are reduced to isolated pools. Some dry up all together. Here the artist has painted fish trapped by receding waters. If the pond does not dry completely, or they do not become prey to birds, the fish will be liberated from their pool when the rains return.

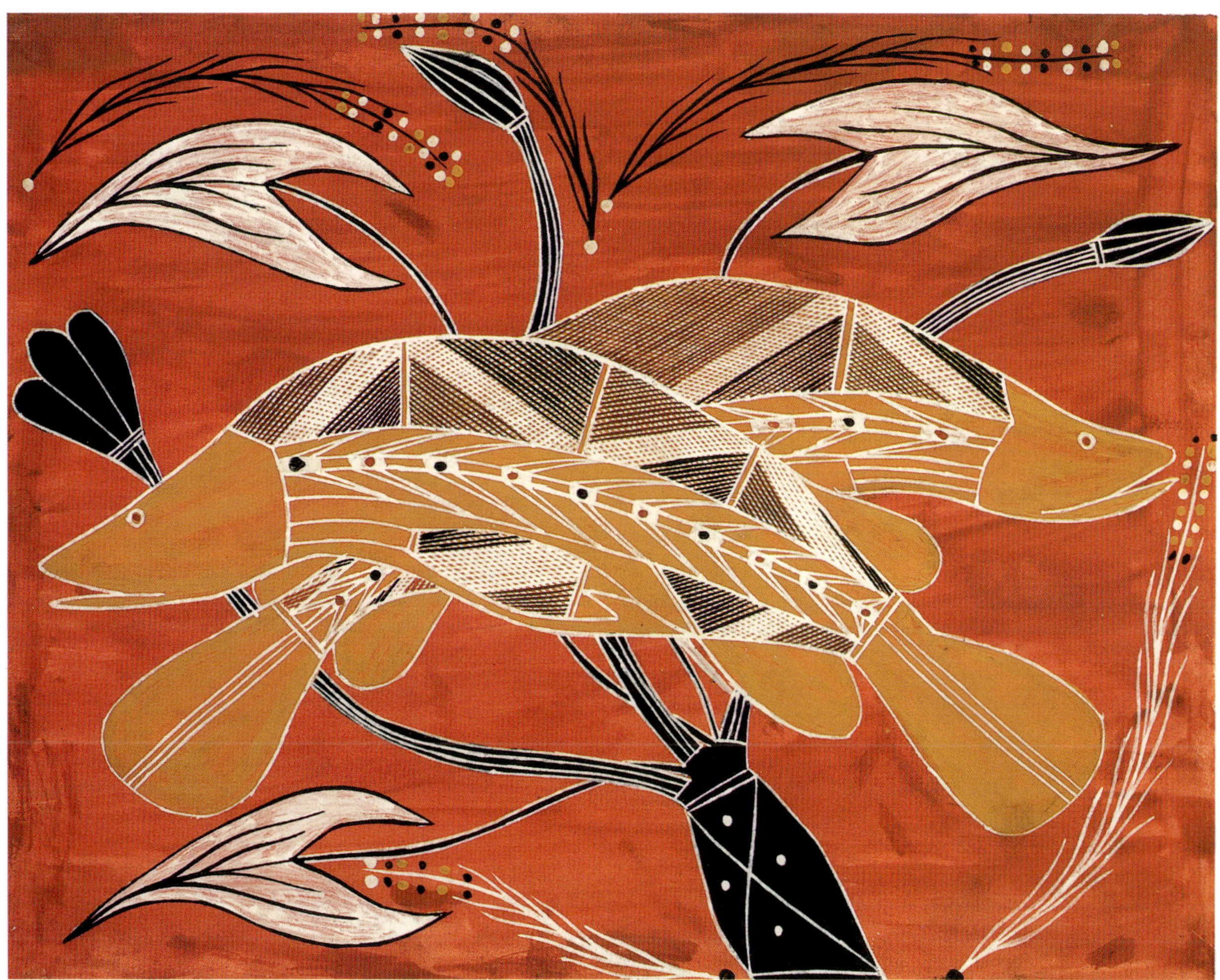

Barramundi, *by David Cameron, 66 x 50 cm*

Here, two barramundi (*namarnkol*) rest below some waterlilies. Lilies are a popular, shady hiding place for this fish. The fish, the bulb and stems of the lilies may be eaten. The artist has done an x-ray likeness of the fish showing its internal structure, including the stomach which is edible.

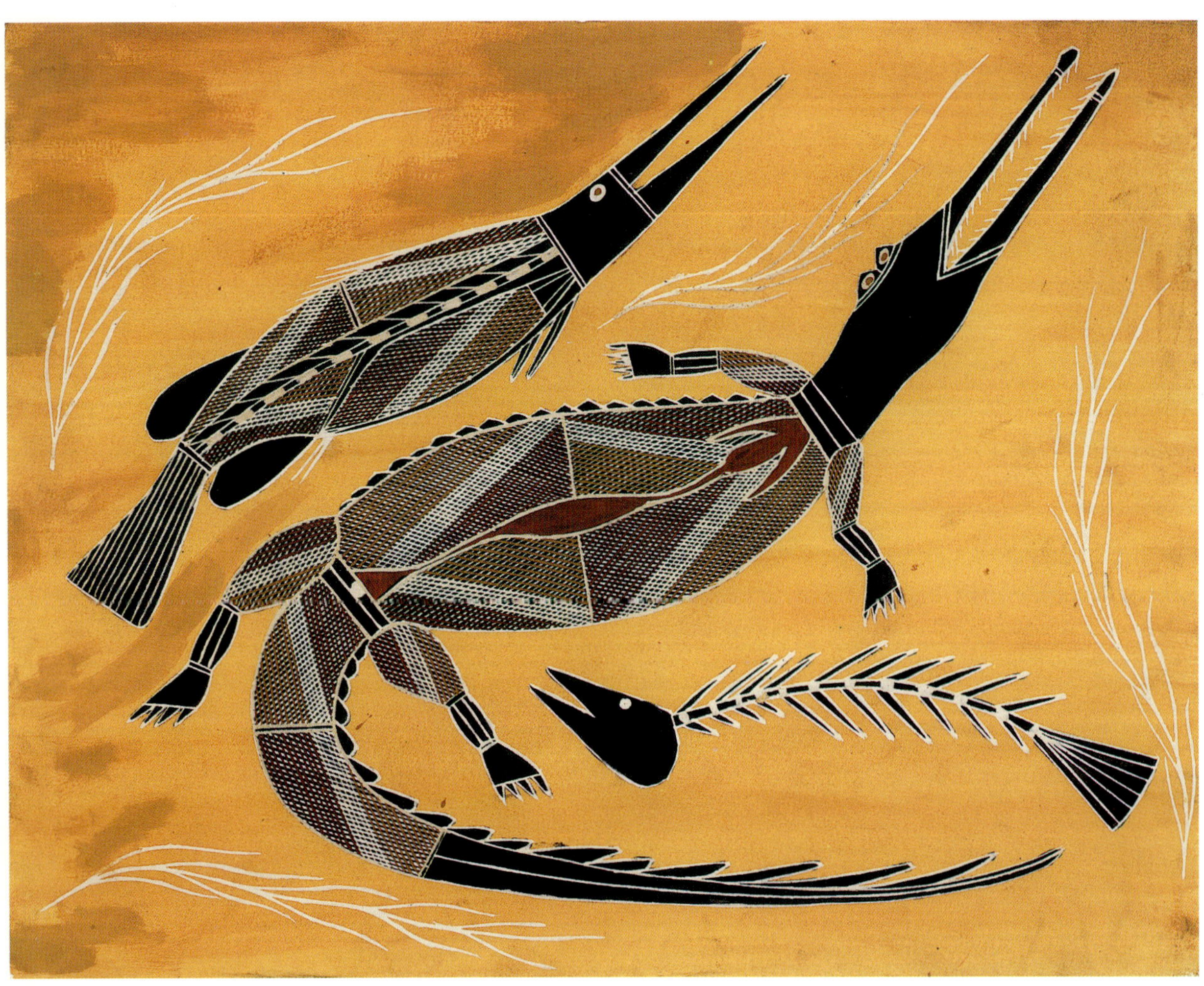

S.H.

Crocodile and Long Tom, *by Danny Djorlom, 66 x 50 cm*

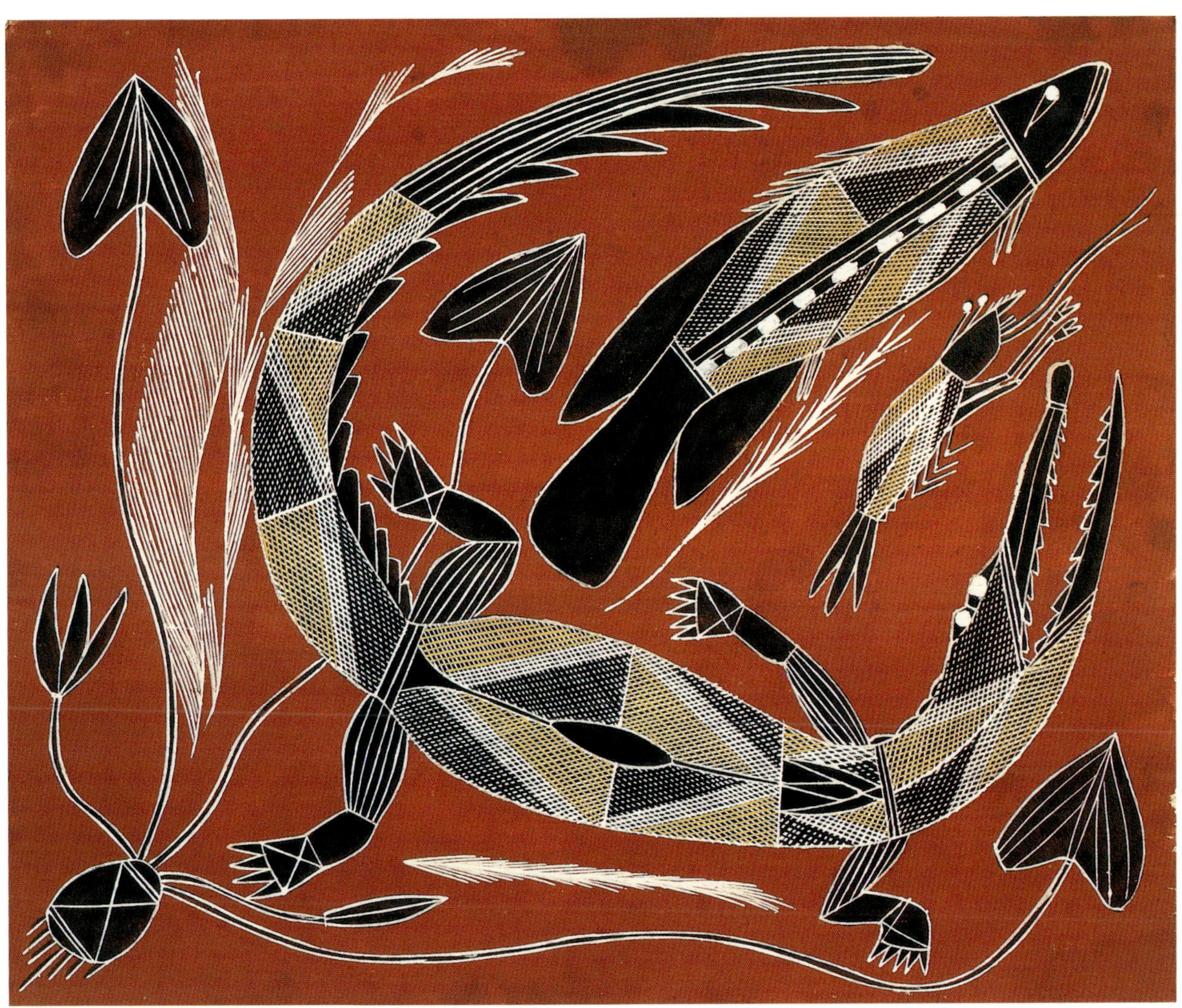

S.H.

Barramundi and Shrimp, *by Danny Djorlom, 66 x 53 cm*

Here the artist has painted the same subject twice with moderate variations. He has depicted both the internal and external structures of the fish. Most artists have subject matter and themes which occur regularly in their work.

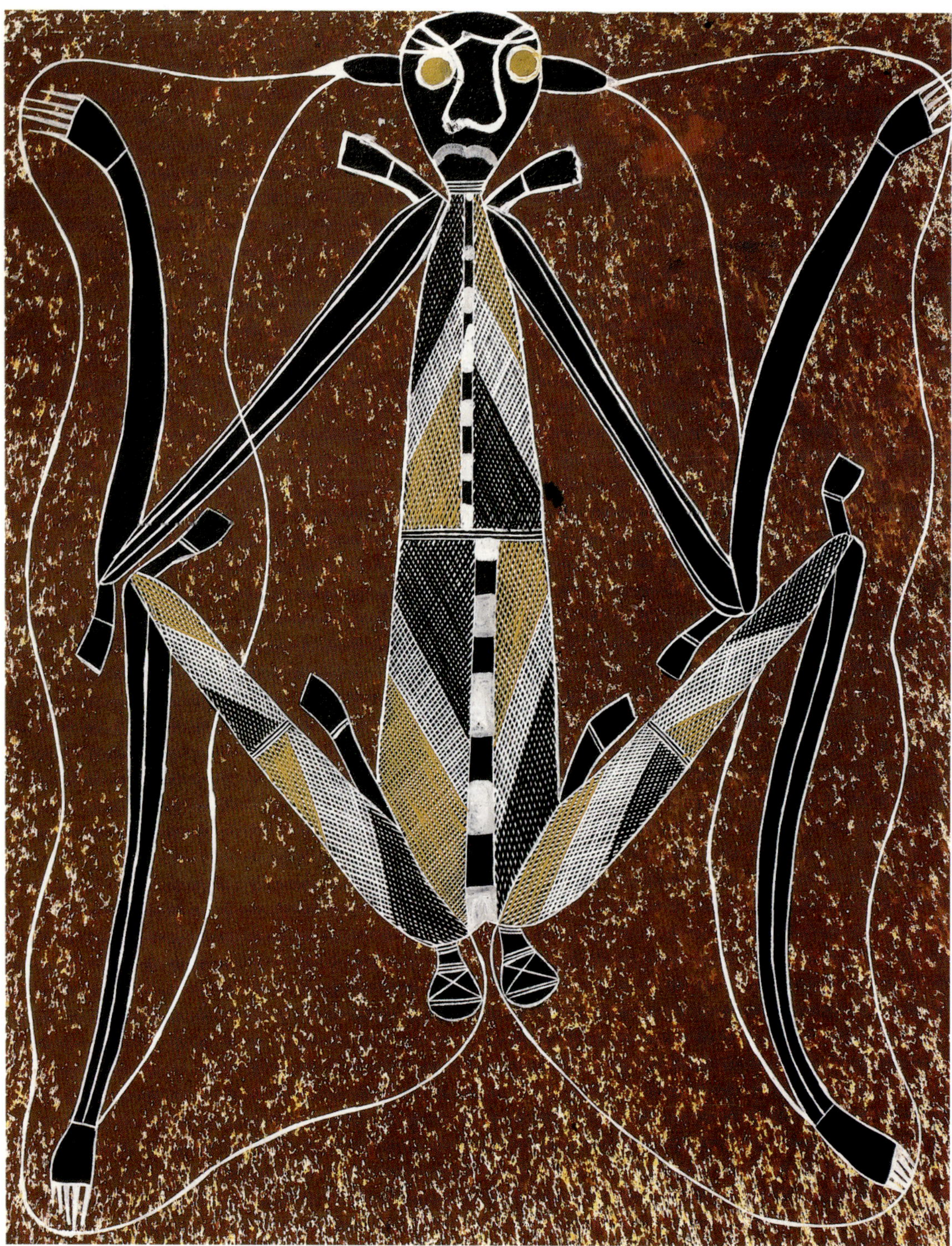

Lightning Man, *by Thompson Nganjmirra, 52 x 66 cm*

Living above the clouds, *Namarrkon* strikes and hurls the stone axes attached to his elbows and knees, when marriage taboos or other aspects of tribal law are broken. His wrath strikes the perpetrators of wrong-doing in the form of lightning. Currents of electricity flow around his body from head to testicles.

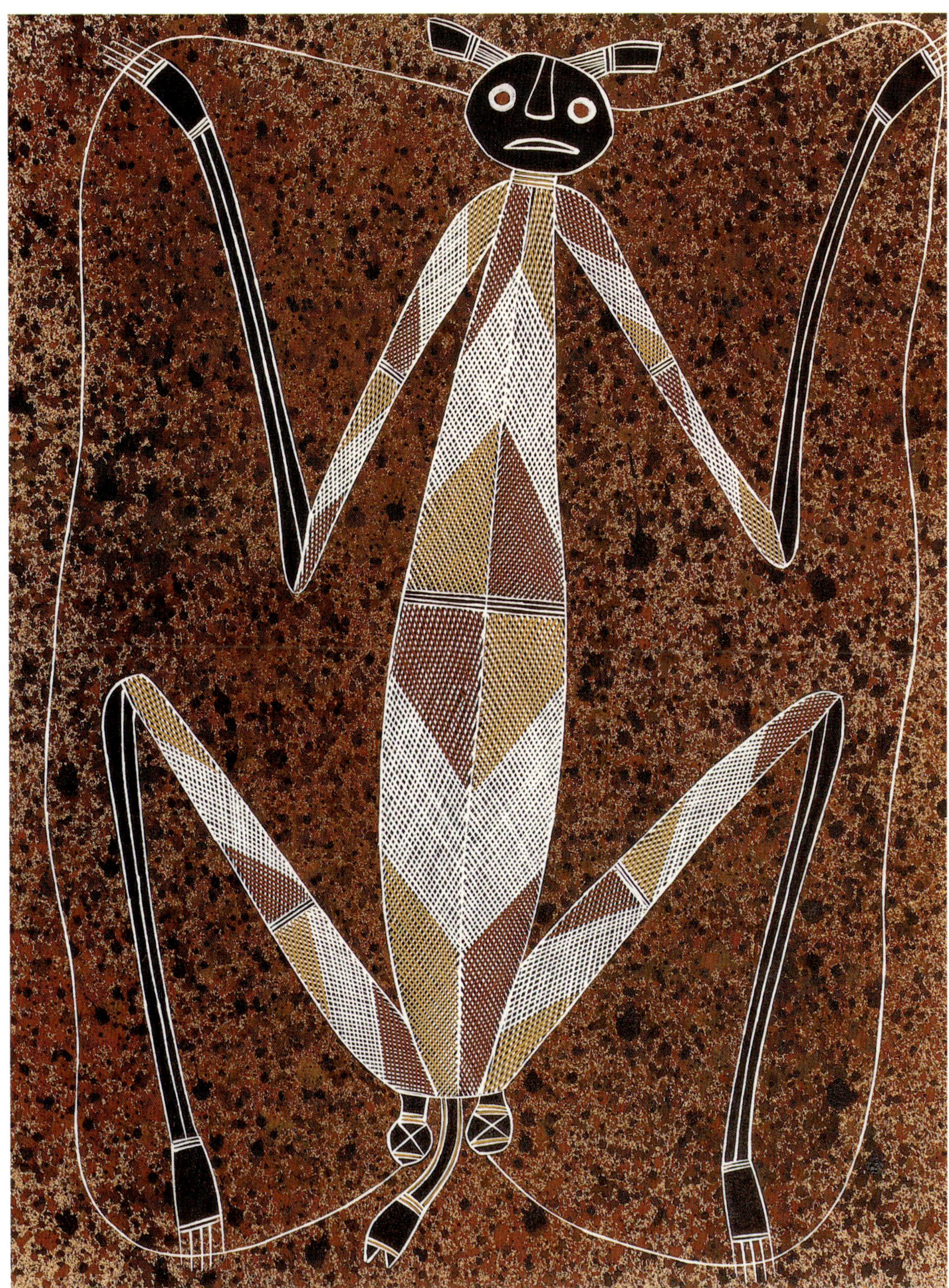

Lightning Man, *by Thompson Nganjmirra, 50 x 66 cm*

This is another example of an artist re-using a theme. Things that the artist enjoys painting and that are important to him are usually reproduced. Again, currents of electricity are flowing between *Namarrkon*'s head and testicles. Split at the head, his penis has been cut open along the shaft.

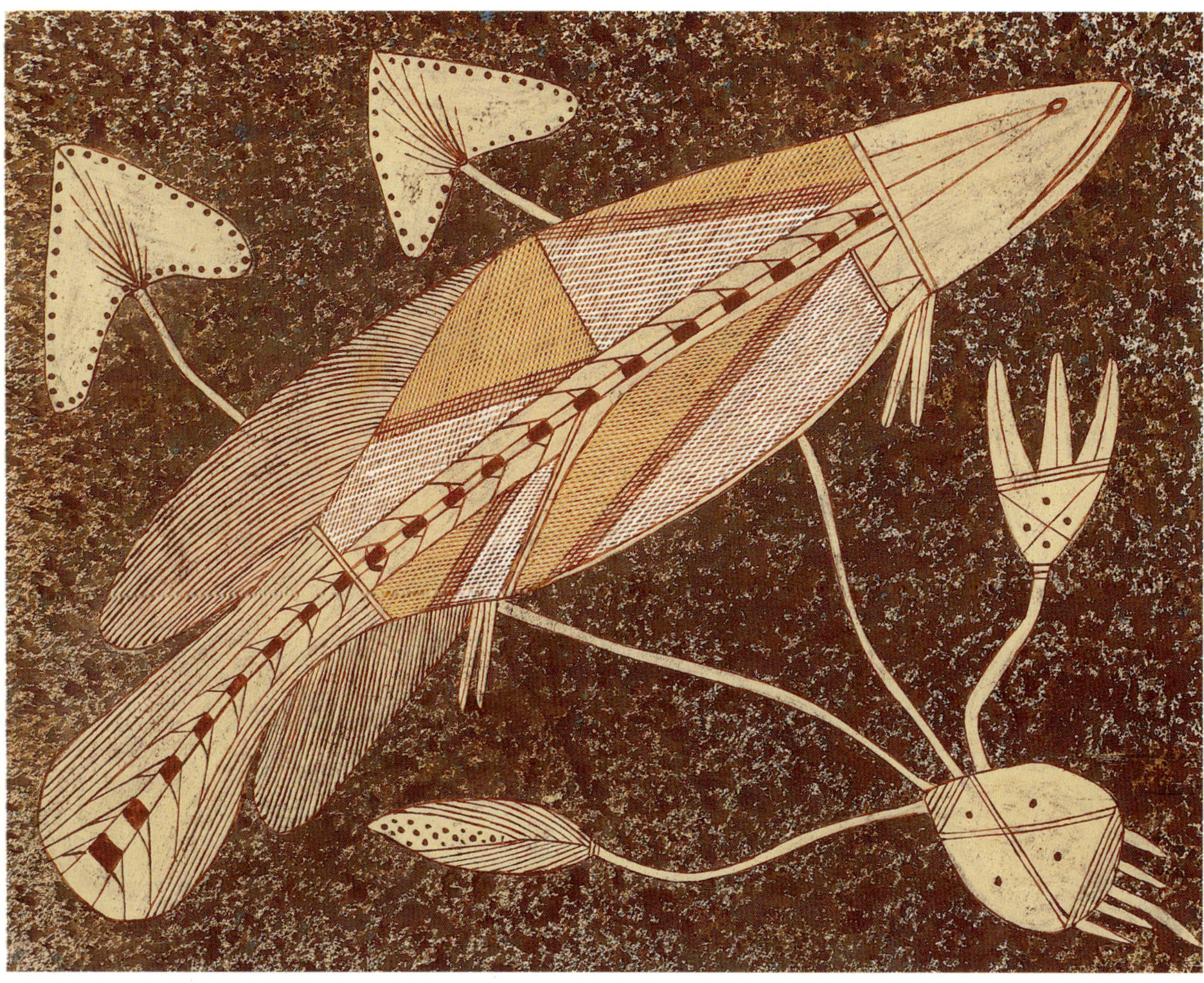

S.H.

Namarnkol, *by Danny Djorlom, 66 x 50 cm*

The great Dreamtime barramundi created much of the country of this artist's clan. As it travelled it created waterholes and billabongs, many of which are sacred (*djang*). Similarly, barramundi is *djang* for the clan and skin group of the artist. The bold, well-shaped lines that decorate the fish are typical of the *Dhuwa* painting style.

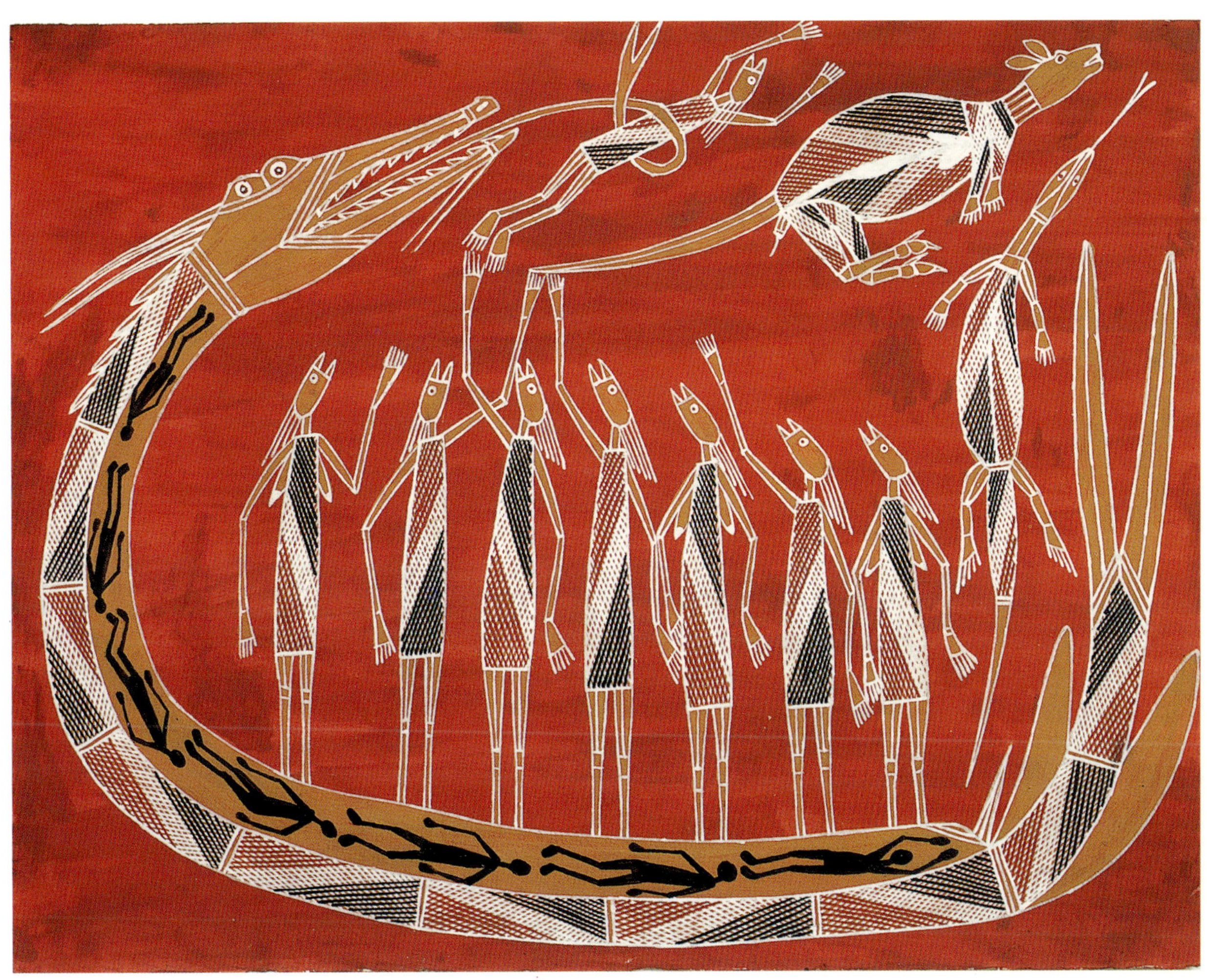

S.H.

Ngalyod Awakens, *by Danny Djorlom, 66 x 51 cm*

This is a story which narrates the awakening of *Ngalyod* in a time since Creation. There was a clan in the Cooper's Creek area in which a group of young mothers had given their babies the wrong food. The children became sick and cried incessantly. Hearing the noise, *Ngalyod* came out of the ground and ate everyone, men, women and babies. The message is that women must take proper care of their children.

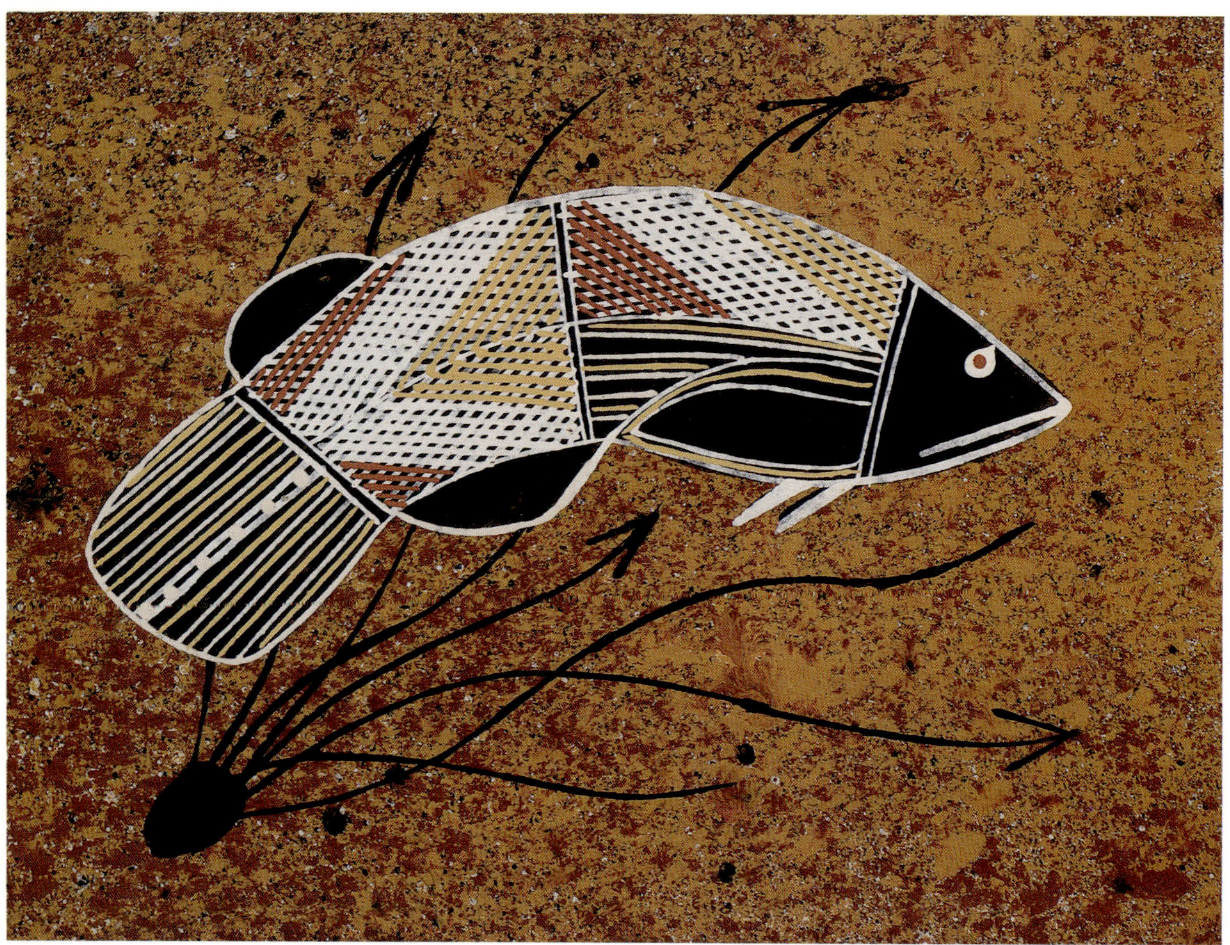

S.H.

Barramundi, *by Alex Nganjmirra, 25 x 19 cm*

This painting contains *rarrk* which is not typical of the artist. Instead of crisscrossing lines,
parallel lines have been used. Others artists, however, often use this style of *rarrk*.

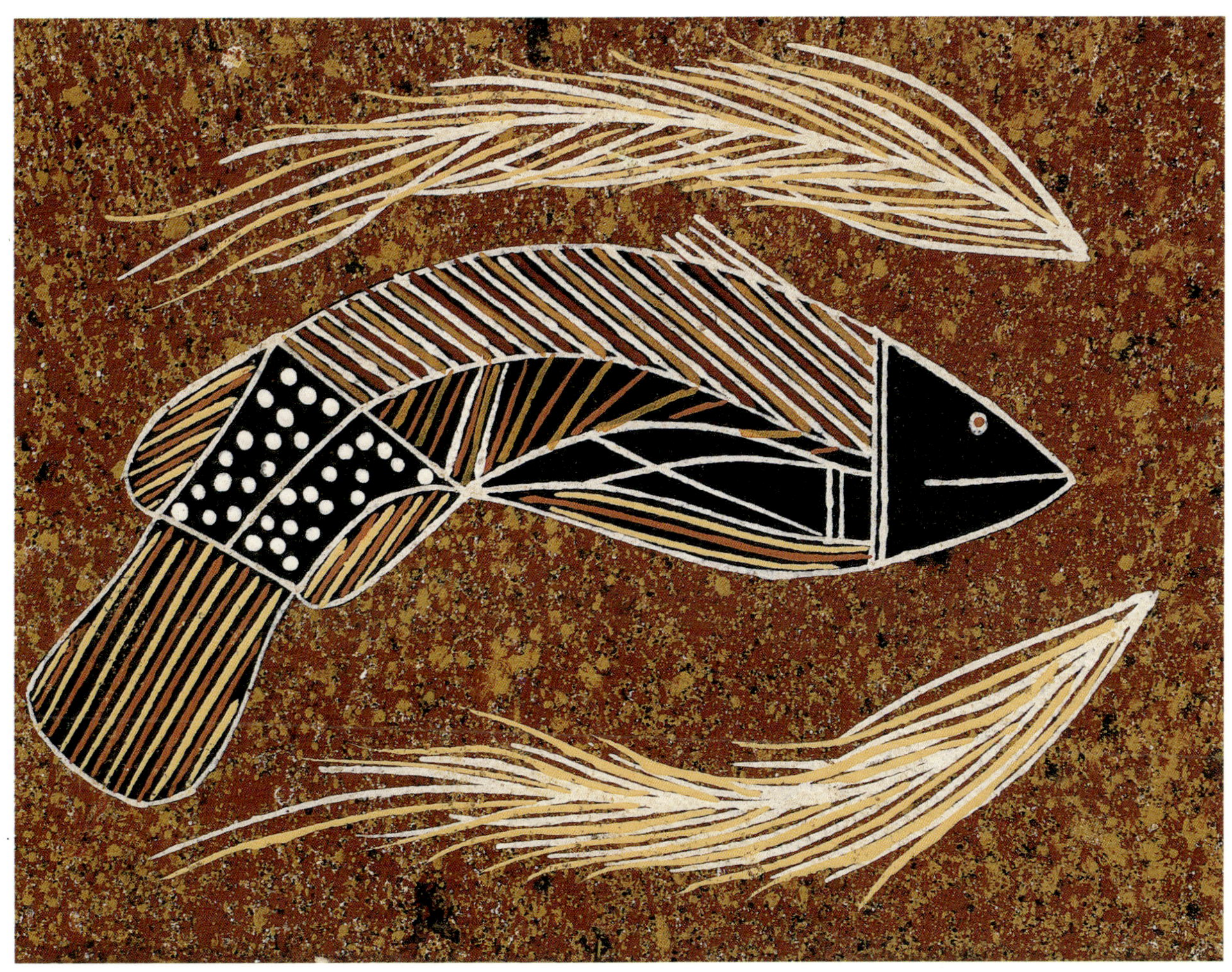

S.H.

Saratoga, *by Alex Nganjmirra, 26 x 19 cm*

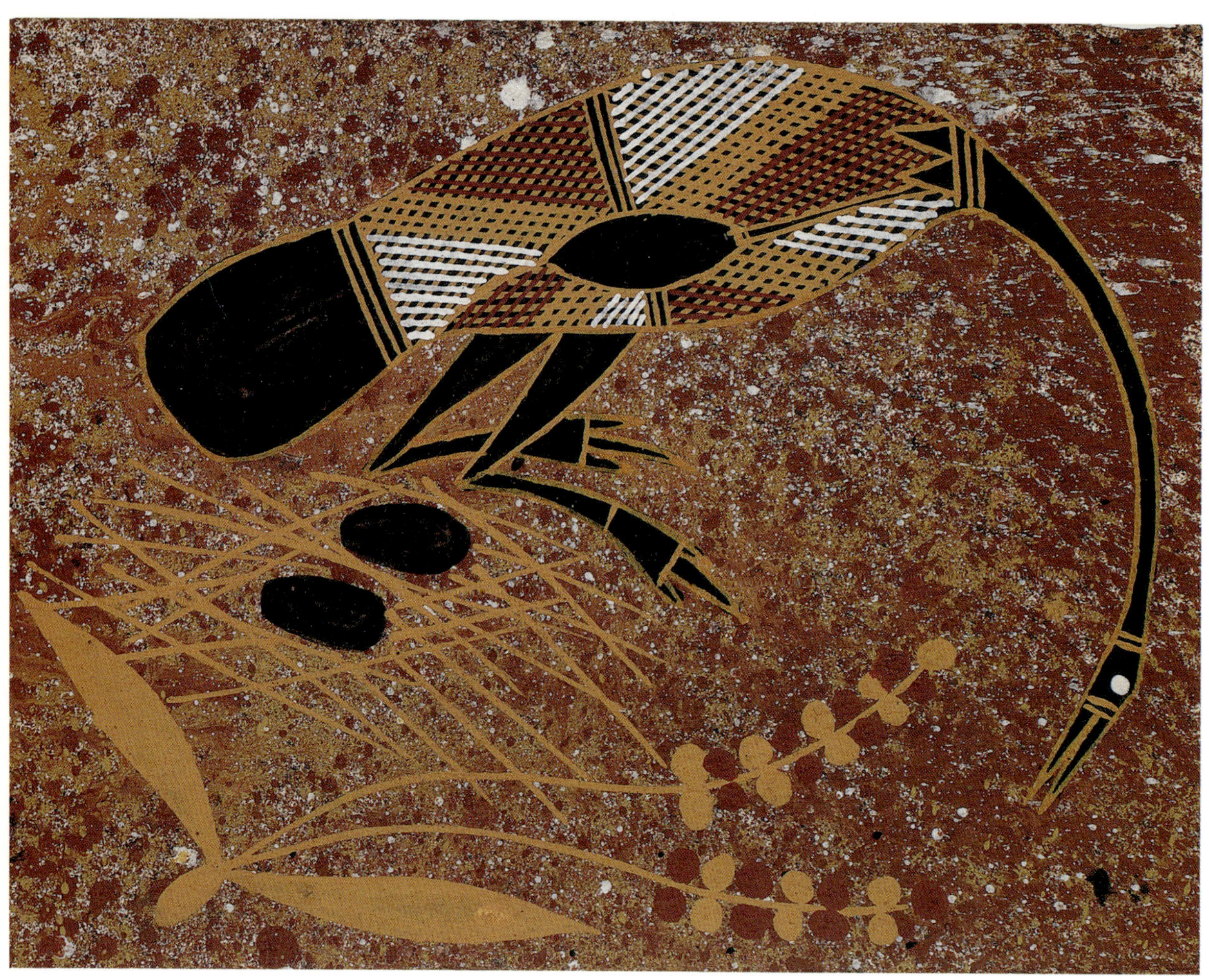

S.H.

Nesting Brolga, *by Mark Nadjongorle, 25 x 19 cm*

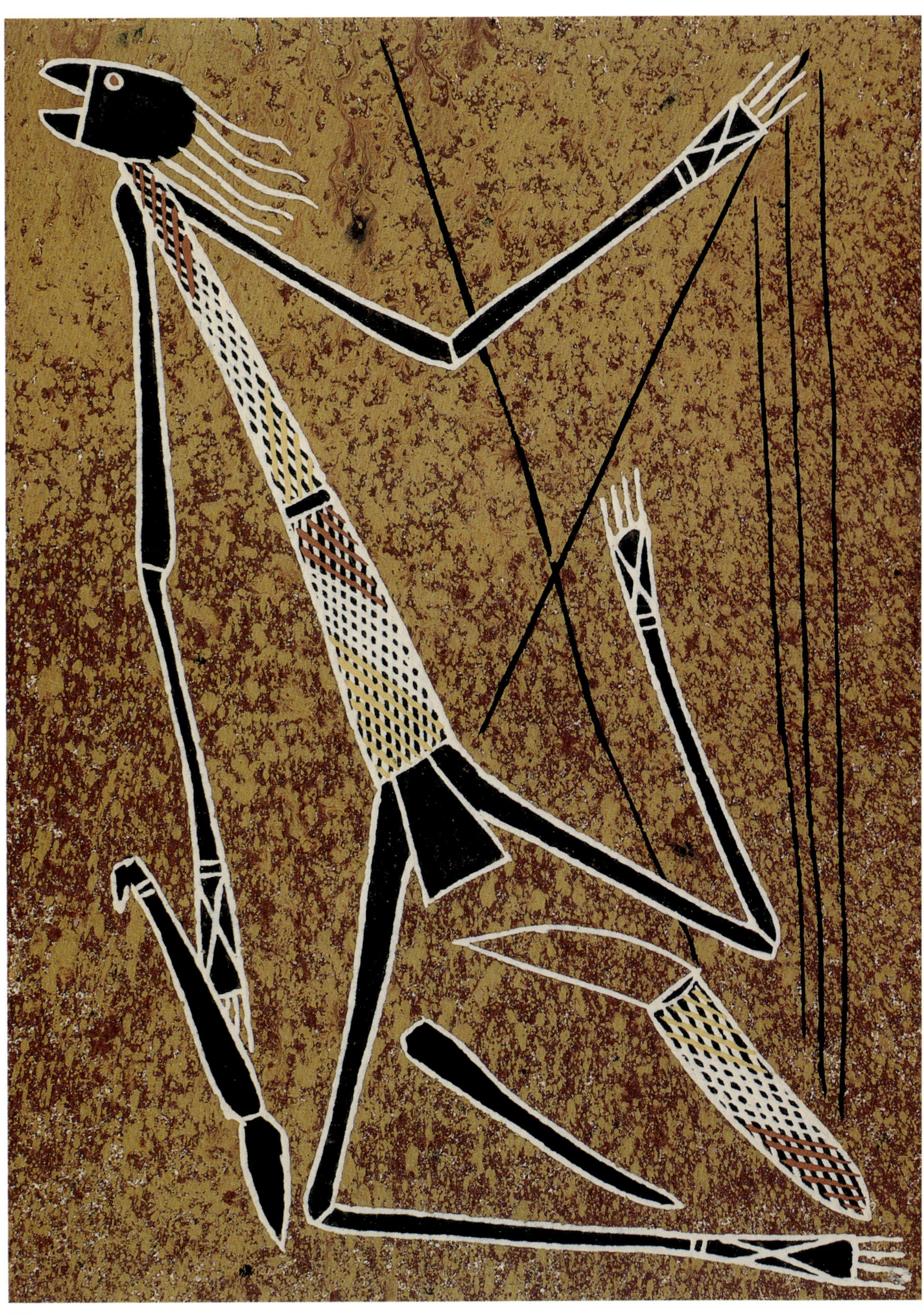

S.H.

Mimi, Hunting Spears, Spear Thrower, Digging Stick and Dilly Bag, *by Alex Nganjmirra, 18 x 26 cm*

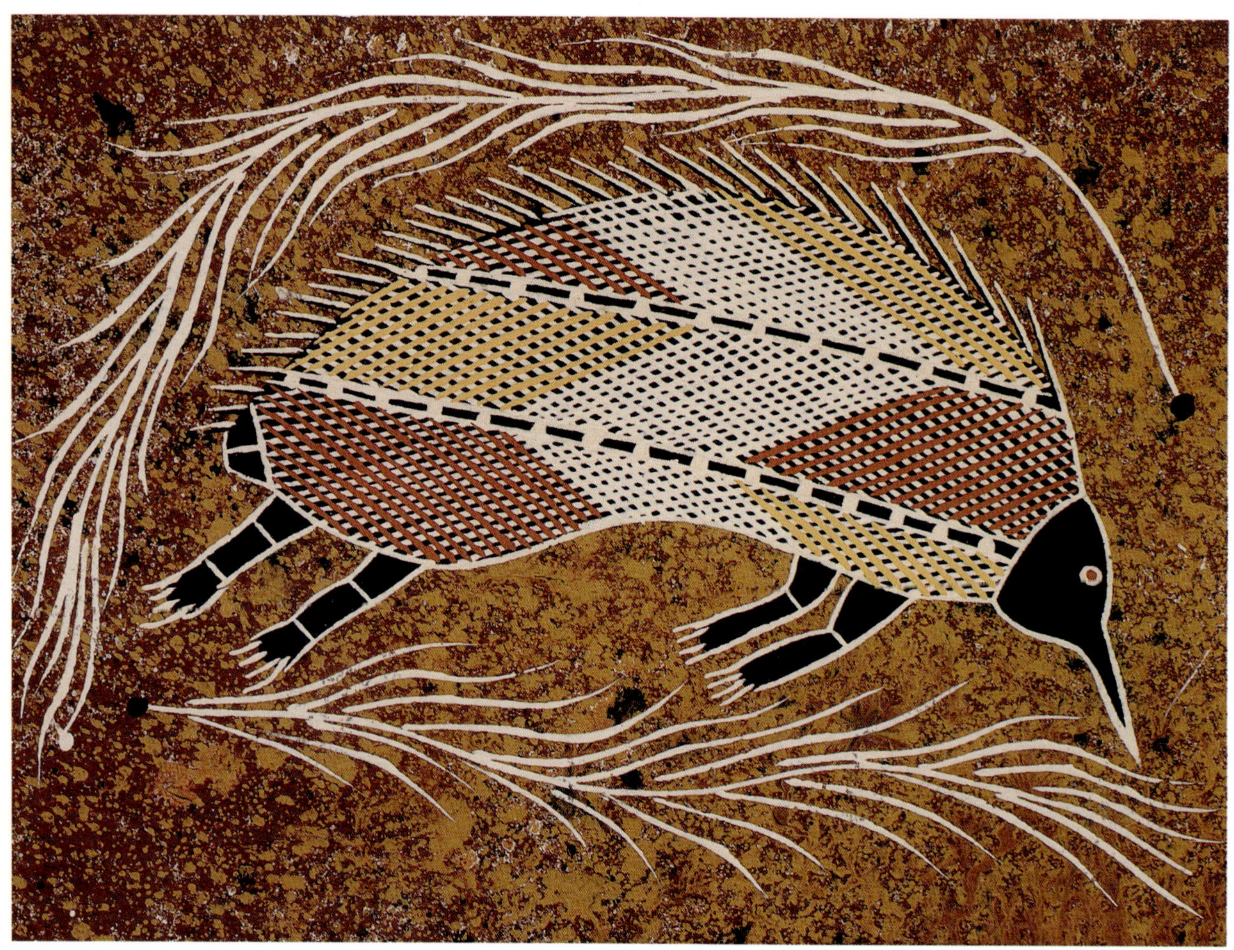

S.H.

Echidna, *by Alex Nganjmirra, 25 x 19 cm*

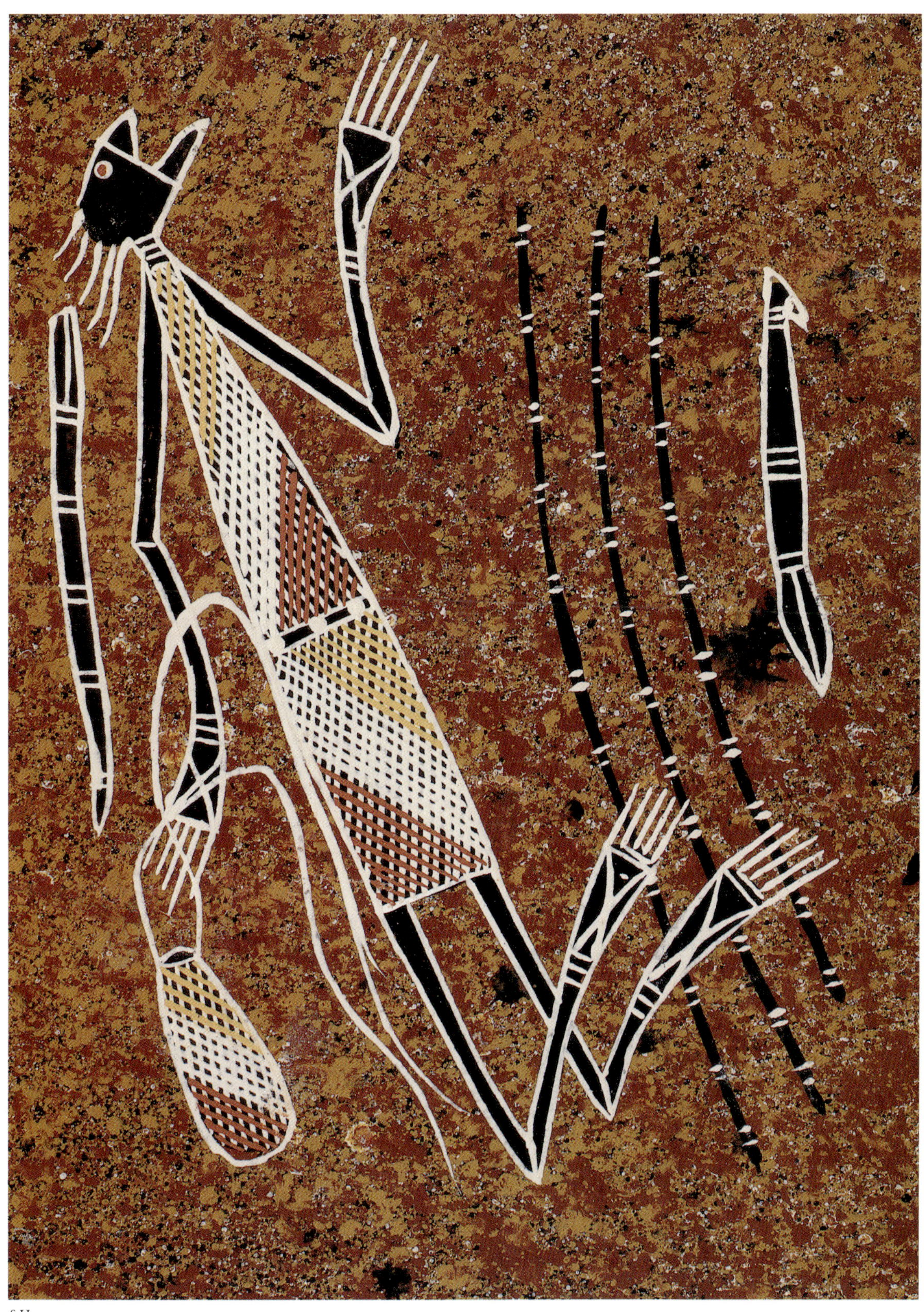

S.H.

Mimi Hunting, *by Alex Nganjmirra, 19 x 26 cm*

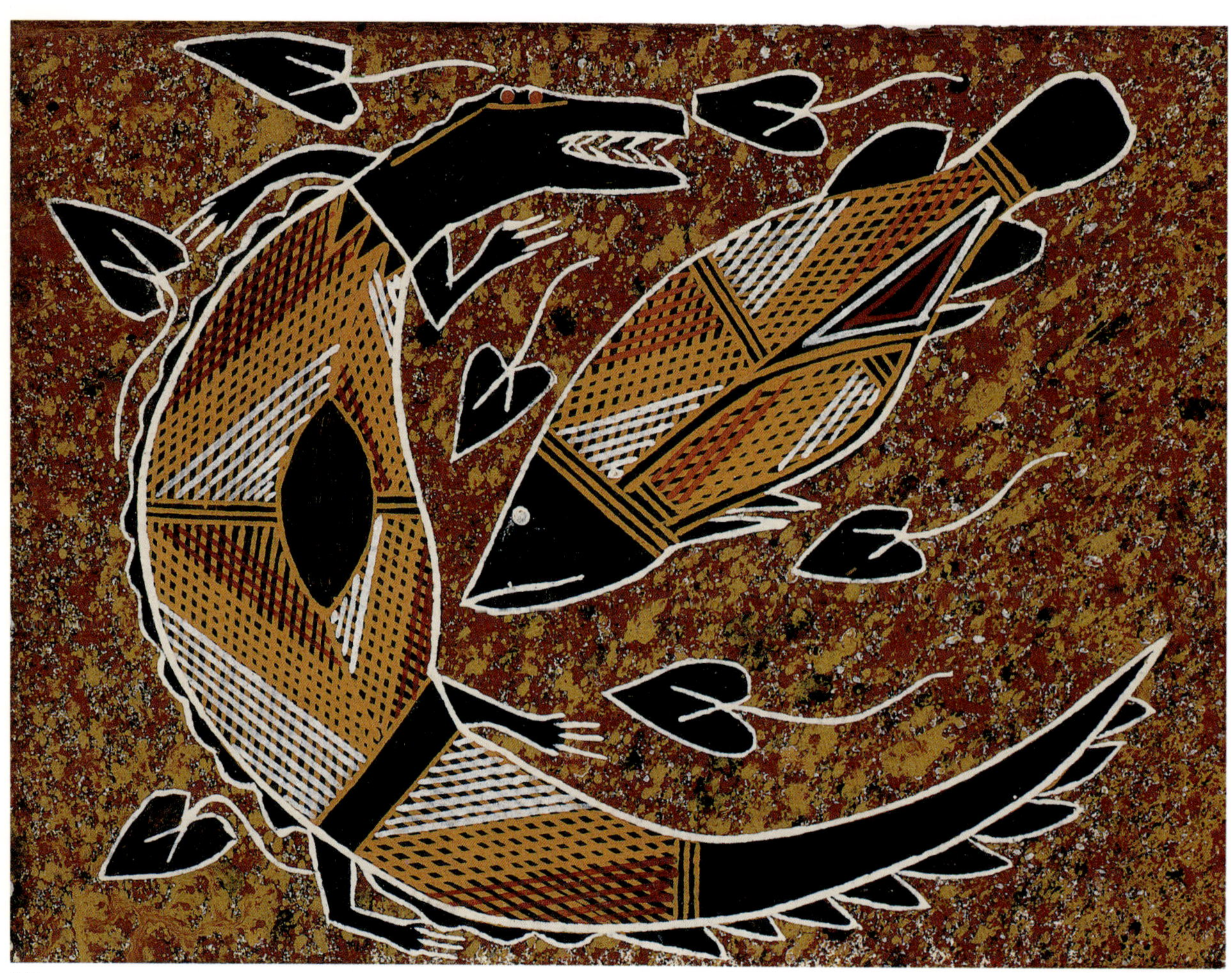

S.H.

Crocodile Preying on Barramundi, *by Alex Nganjmirra, 26 x 19 cm*

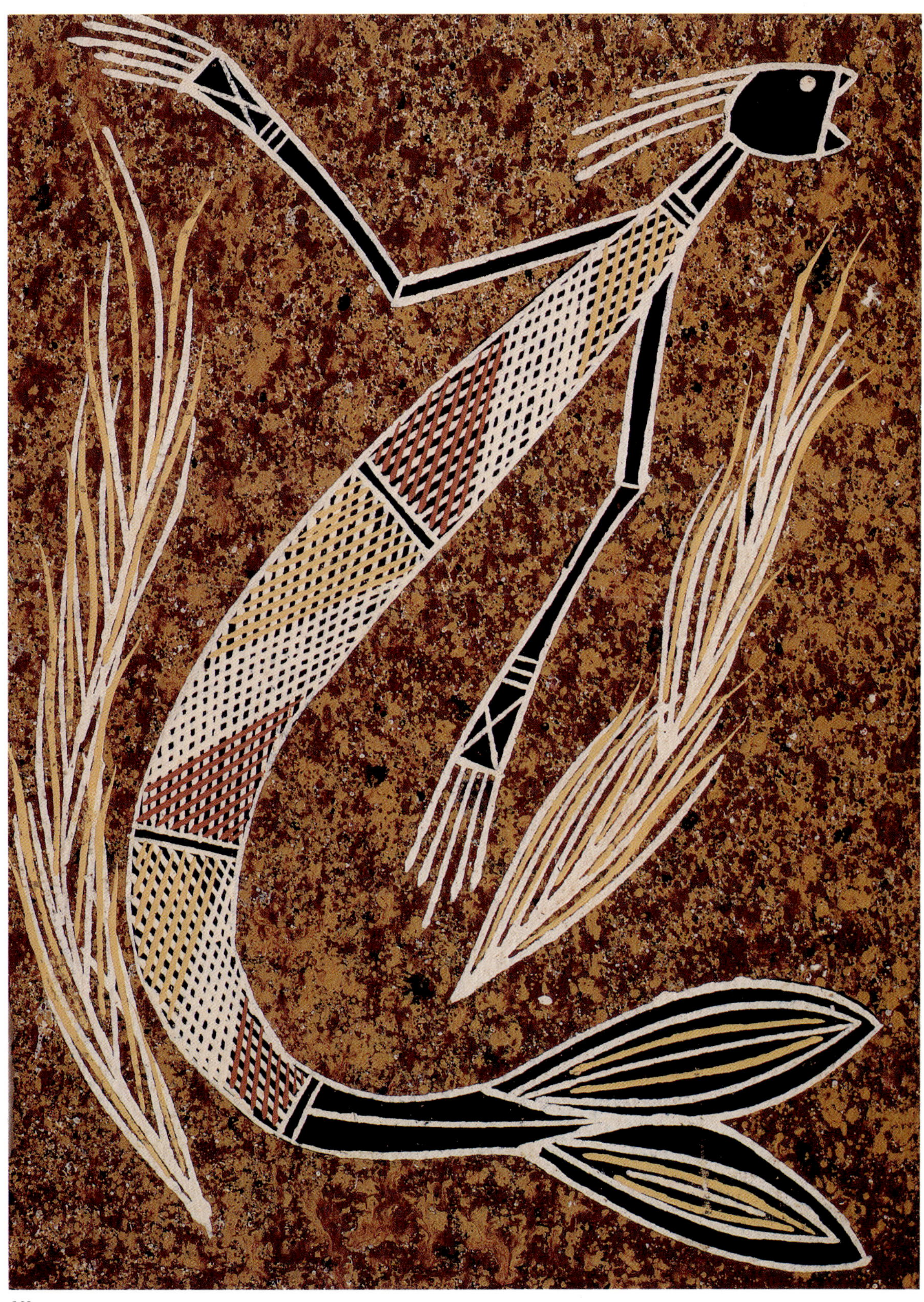

Freshwater Mermaid *(Yawk Yawk), by Alex Nganjmirra, 19 x 25 cm*

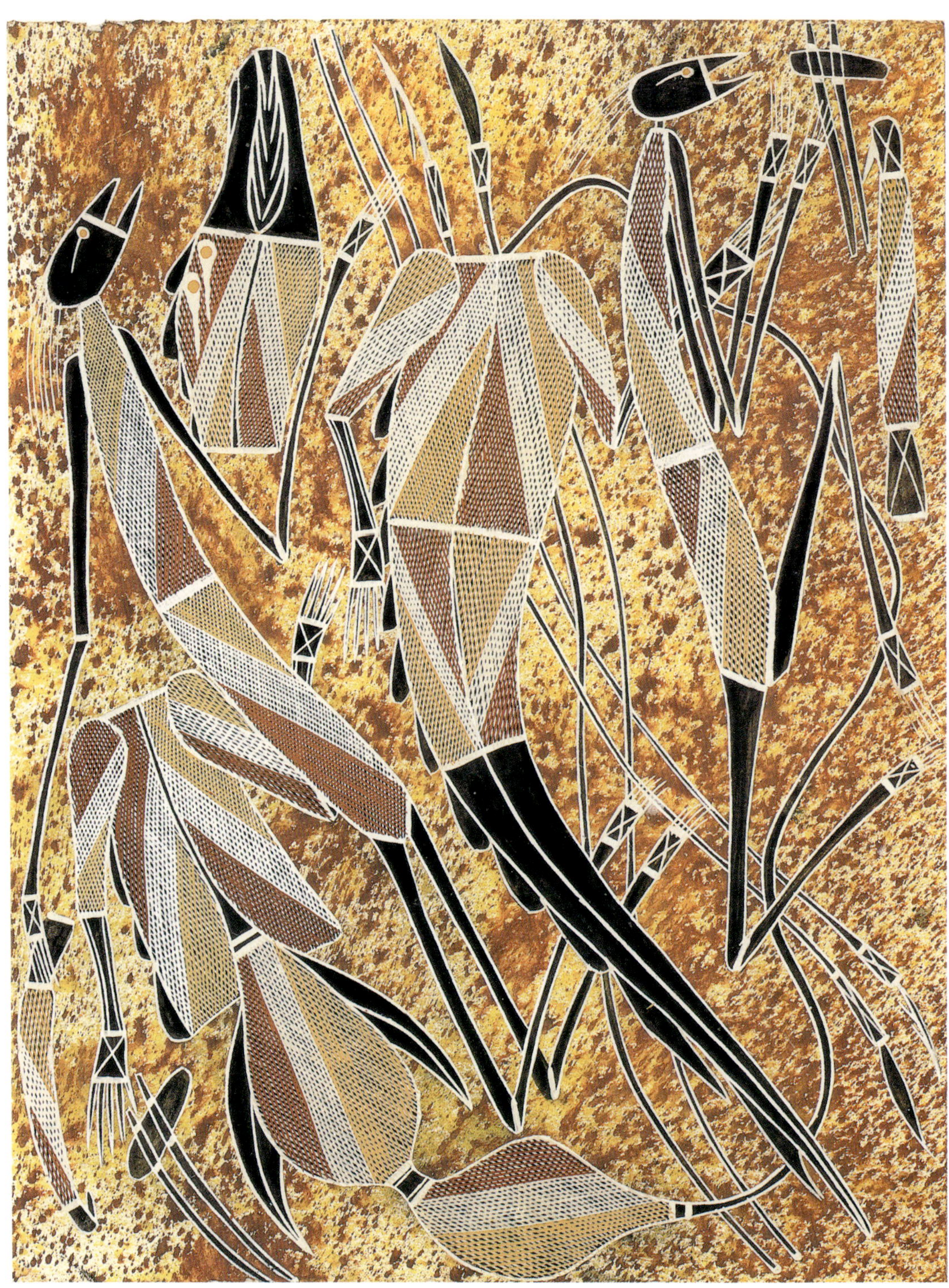

Dismembered Crocodile, *by Abraham Dakgalawuy, 51 x 66 cm*

This painting contains two *Mimi* who have killed and dissected a saltwater crocodile (*ginga*). The hunters are equipped with spears, spear throwers and stone axes. With its head hacked from its body, the crocodile lies with its entrails surrounding the hunters. Kunwinjku artists often illustrate methods of dissecting common foods.

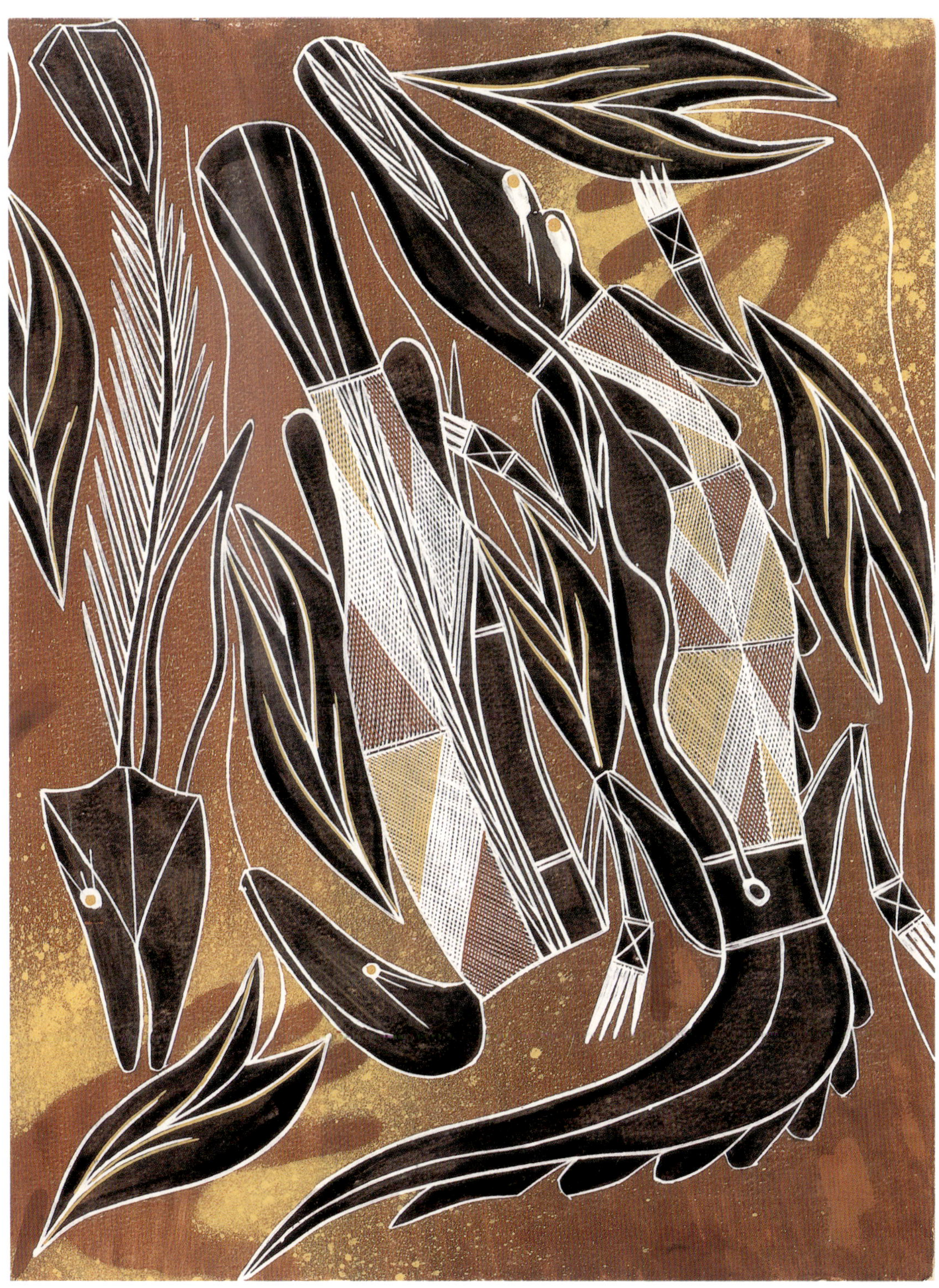

Feeding Crocodile, *by Abraham Dakgalawuy, 66 x 50 cm*

Here a saltwater crocodile lays ready to consume a barramundi it has just killed. The crocodile has caught the fish, flicking his tail to snap the fish's neck. The remains of a previously consumed fish lie next to it.

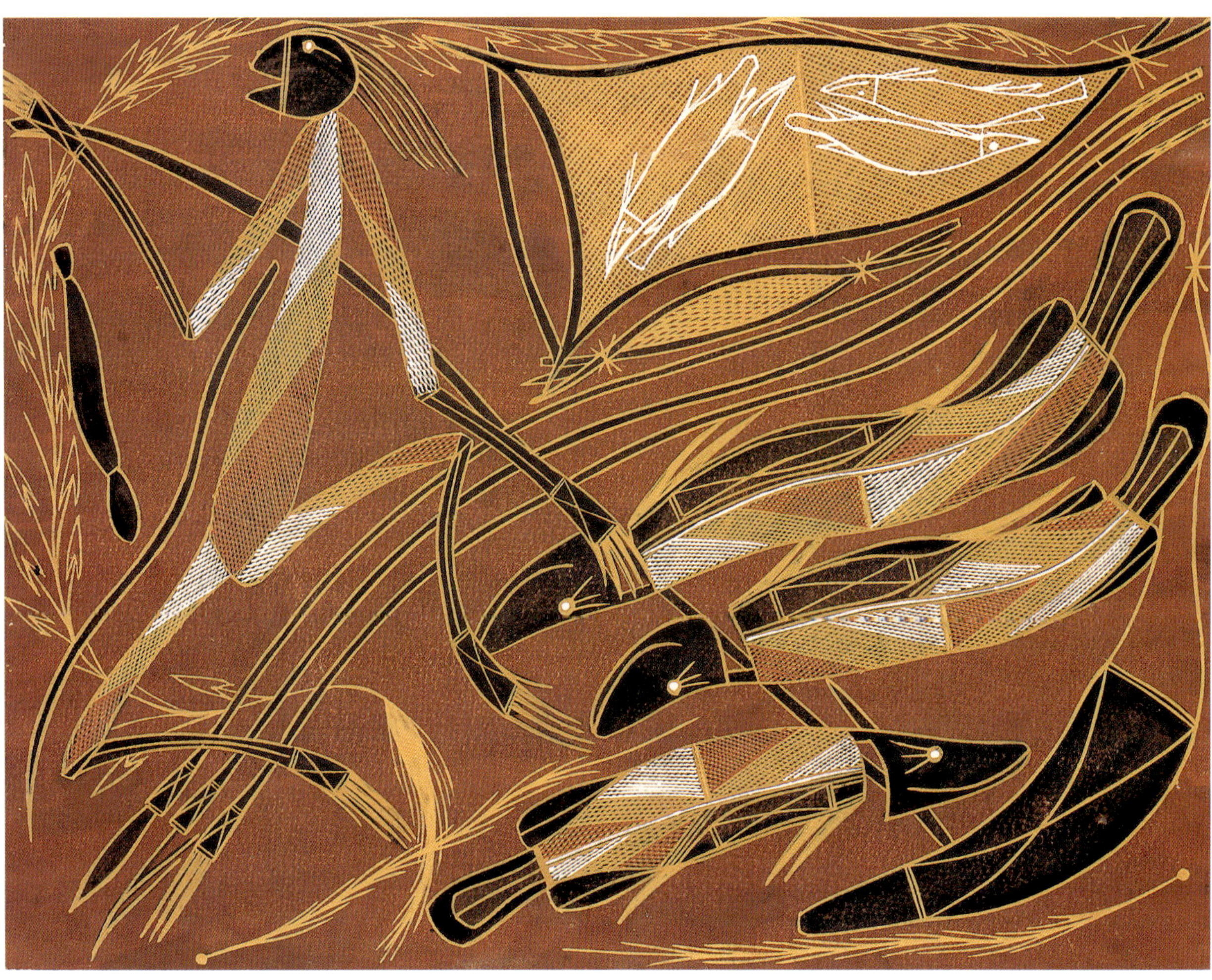

S.H.

Man Fishing, *by Abraham Dakgalawuy, 66 x 51 cm*

In this painting a *Binninj* man is catching fish the traditional way. He is using a woven fish trap
and spears. Fish lie caught within the trap while outside it the fresh catch lies upside down,
indicating that it is dead. A dilly bag waits to be filled with the catch.

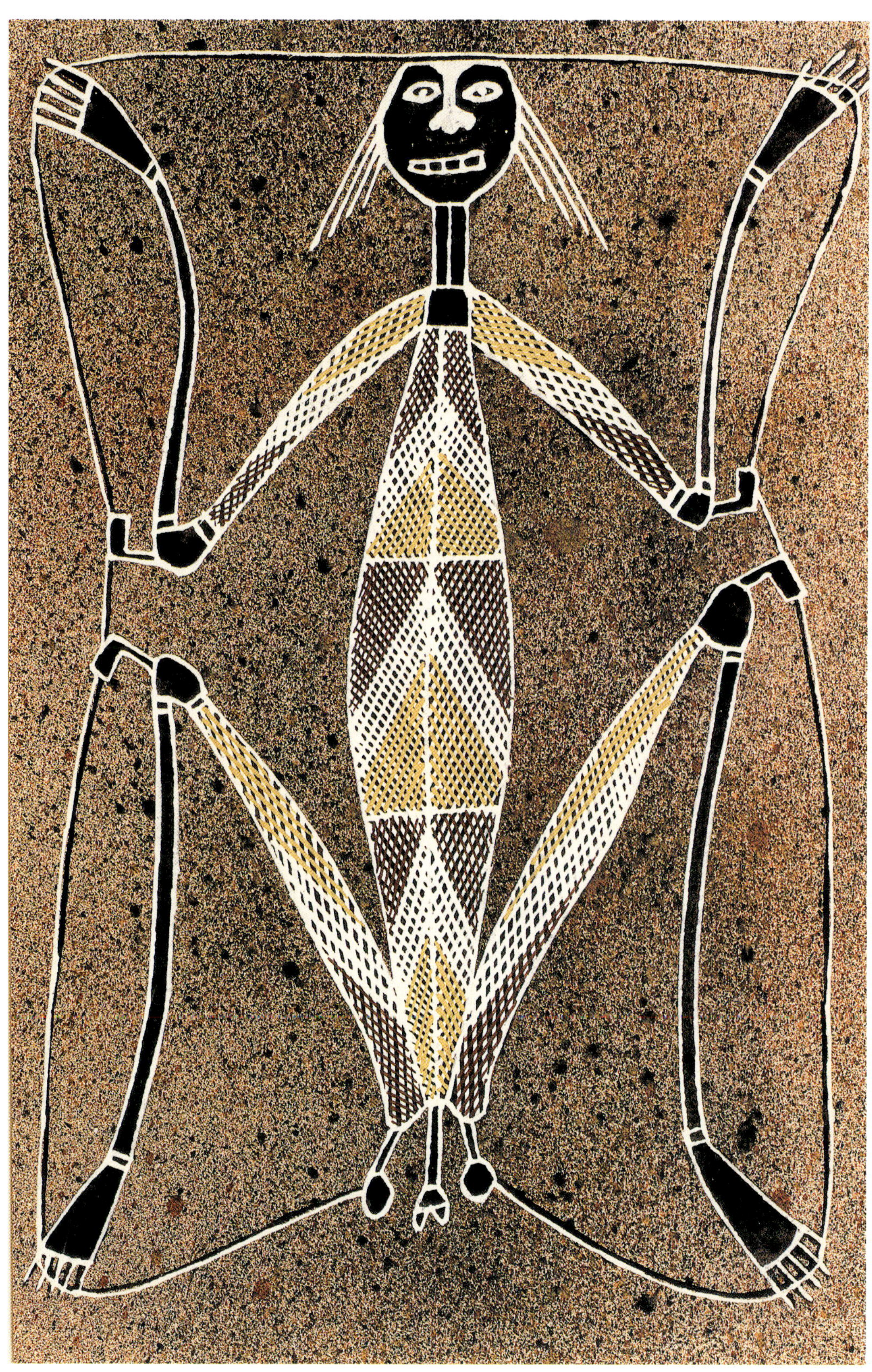

Namarnkoi, *by Danny Djorlom, 26 x 40 cm*

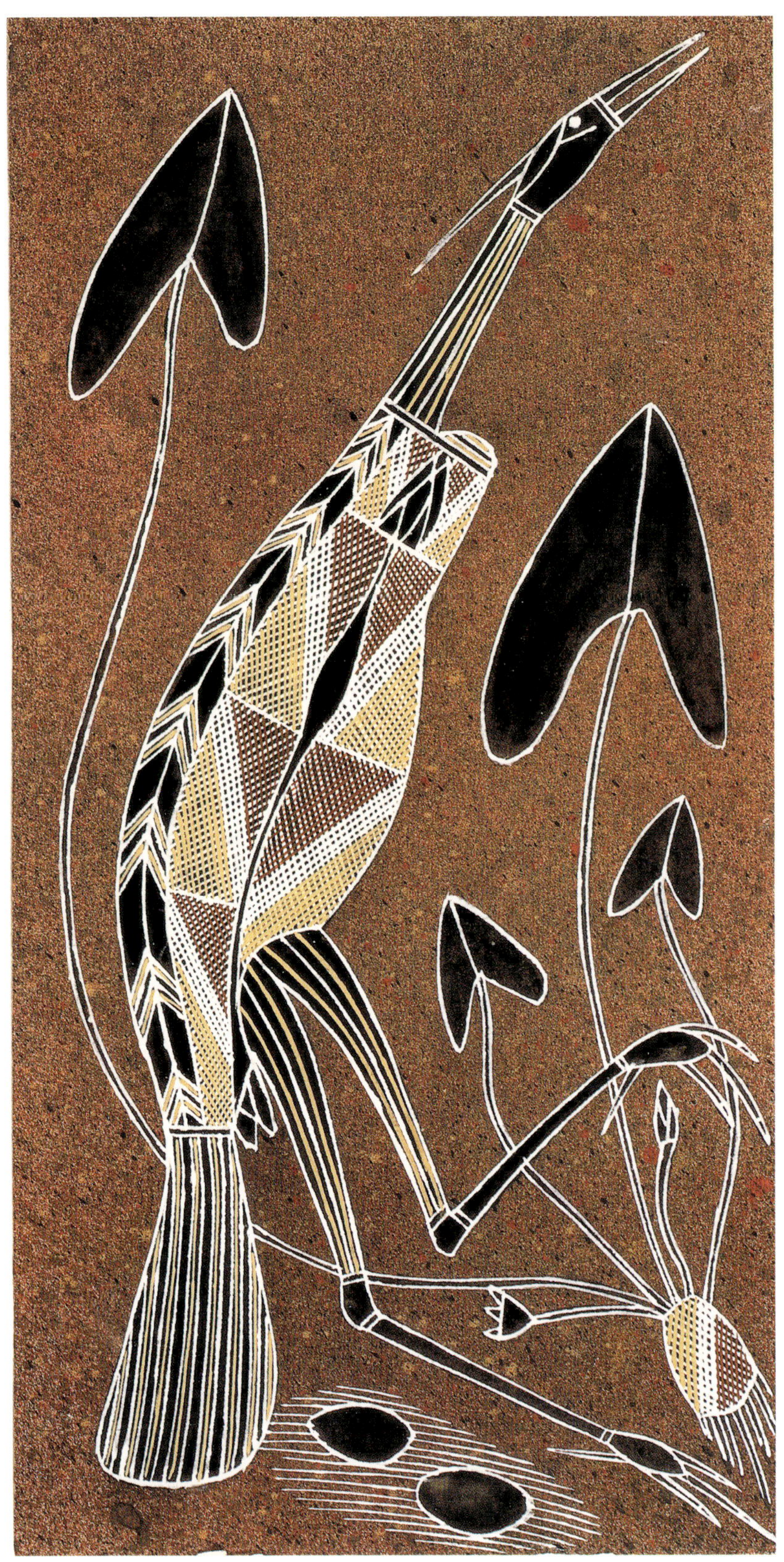

S.H.

Pied Heron, *by Danny Djorlom, 34 x 67 cm*

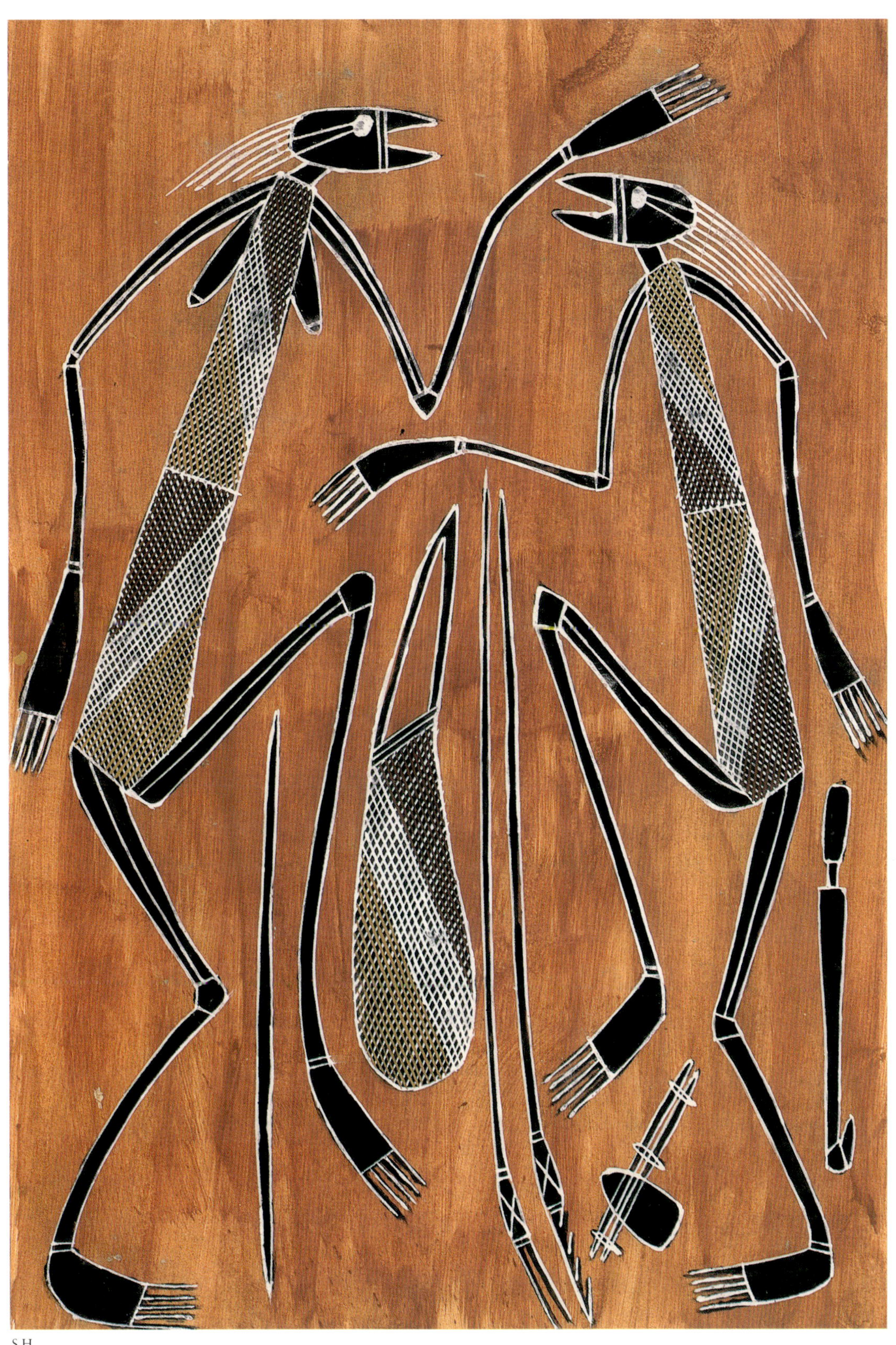

S.H.

Mimi Spirits Dancing, *by Trevor Nganjmirra, 38 x 56 cm*

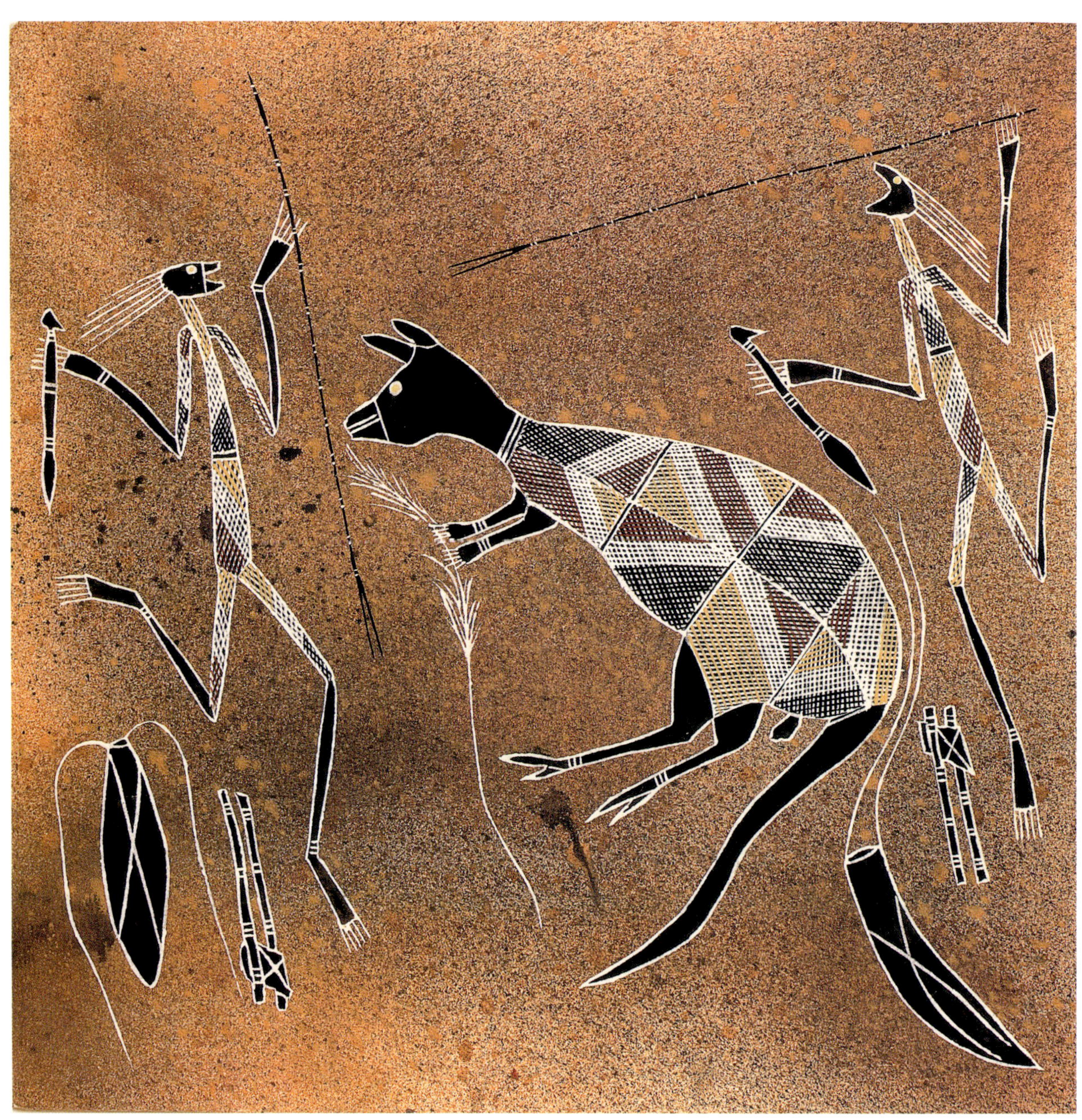

Mimi Men Hunting, *by John Lemibanda, 52 x 51 cm*

Mimi spirits, through dream and instruction, taught *Binninj* people to hunt. Along with Luma they are also credited with teaching them to paint. During the Dreamtime, some stories referred to giant kangaroos. Archaeological digs have shown that large, slow moving, kangaroo-like animals once existed in these parts, but were hunted to extinction. In this painting *Mimi* spirits hunt a giant kangaroo while it feeds.

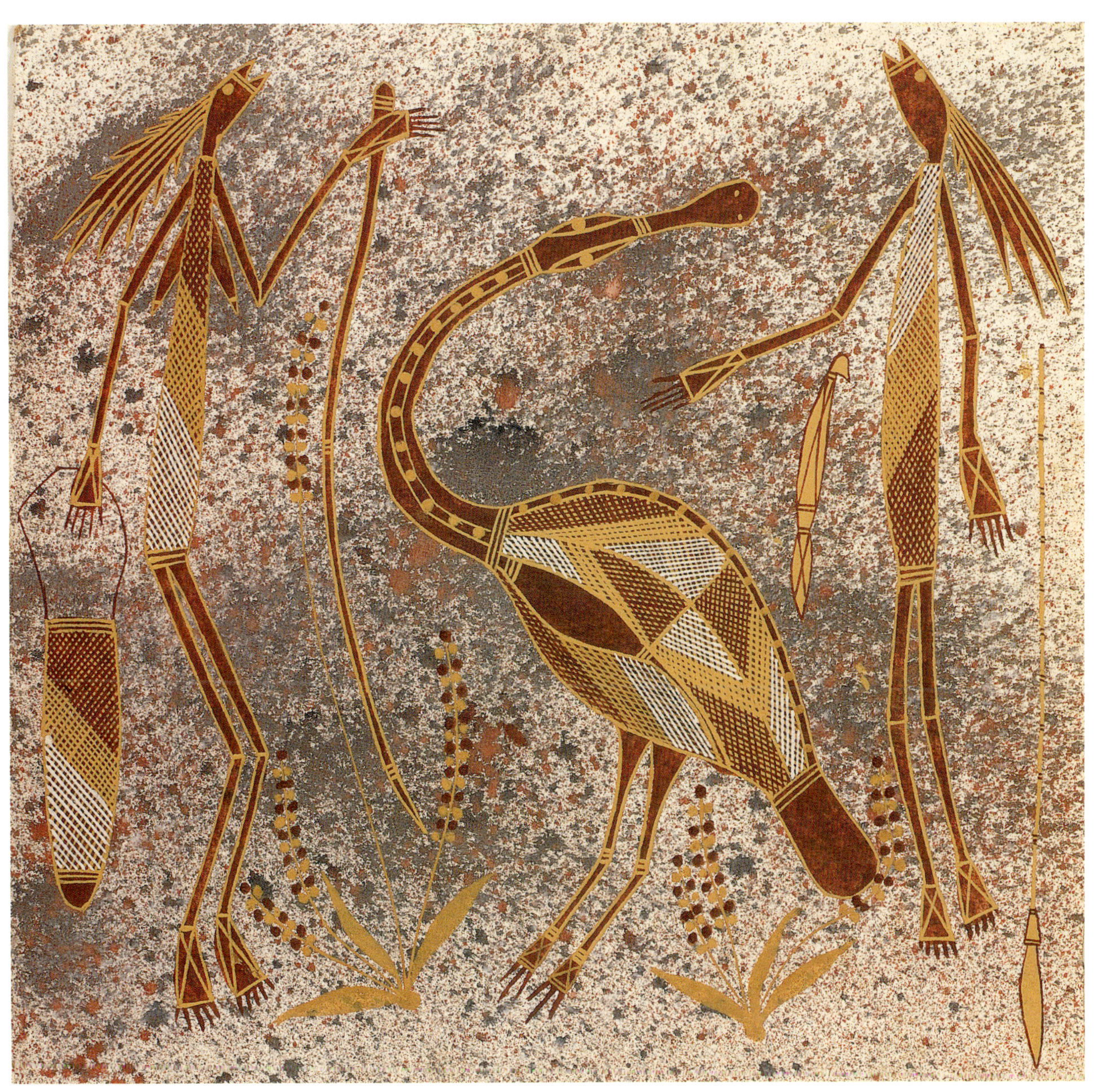

S.H.

Spoonbill, *by Joshua Bangar, 52 x 51 cm*

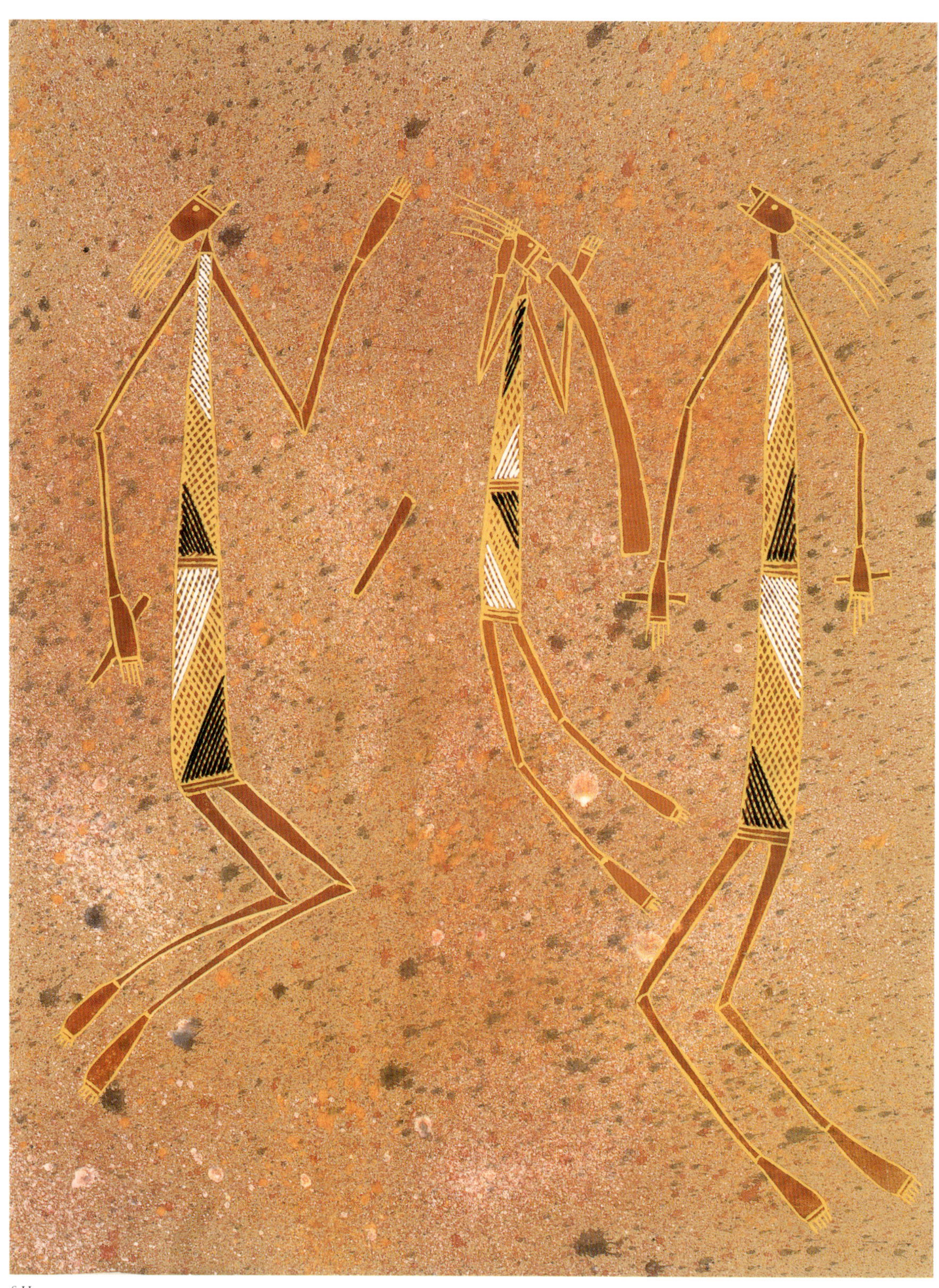

Making Music, *by Alex Nganjmirra, 38 x 50 cm*

Bilk Bilk taught the Kunwinjku people music. Here two *Binninj* men can be seen playing clap-
sticks, dancing and singing to the music of the didgeridoo.

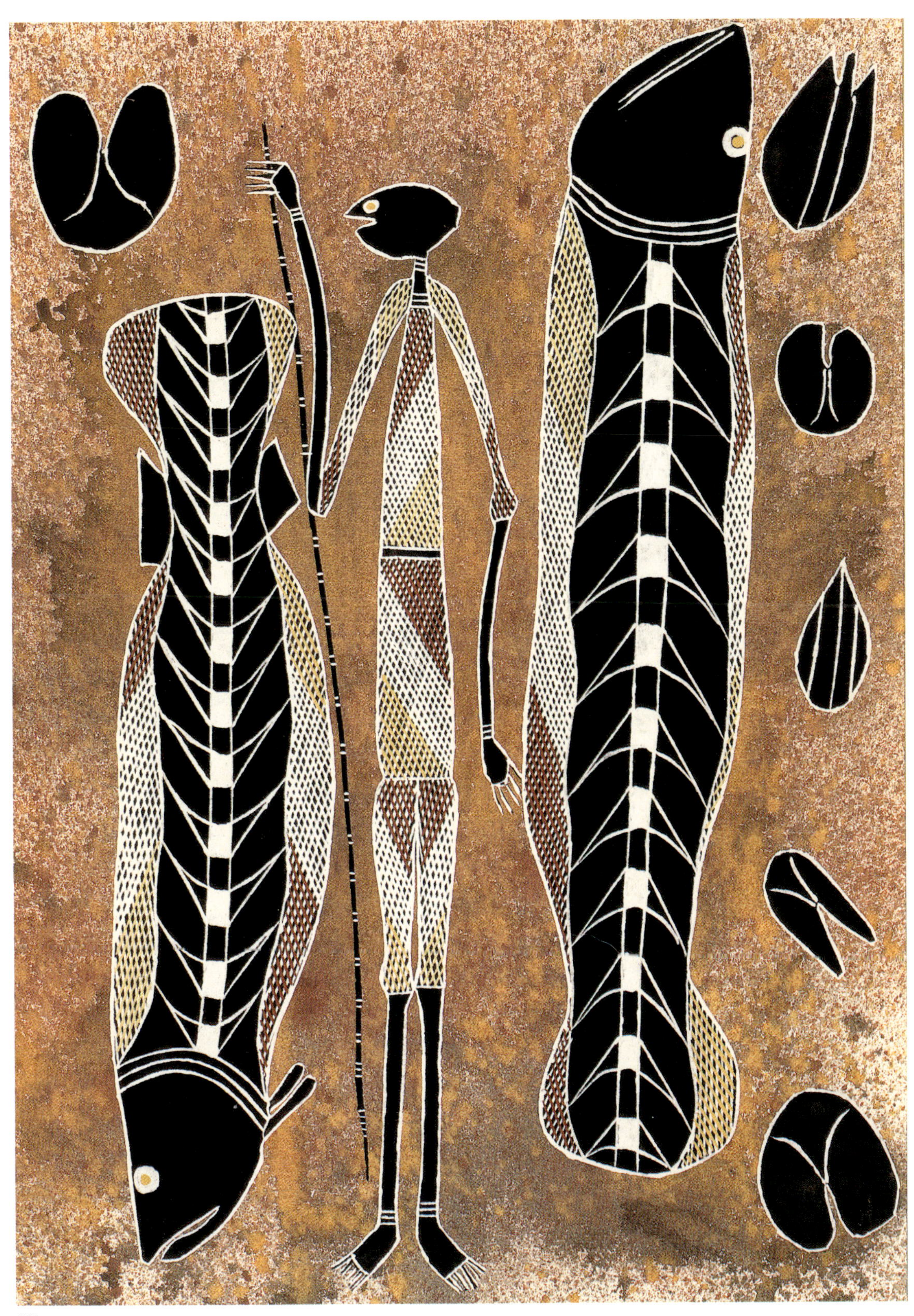

Fishermen with Saratoga, *by Alex Nganjmirra, 38 x 50 cm*

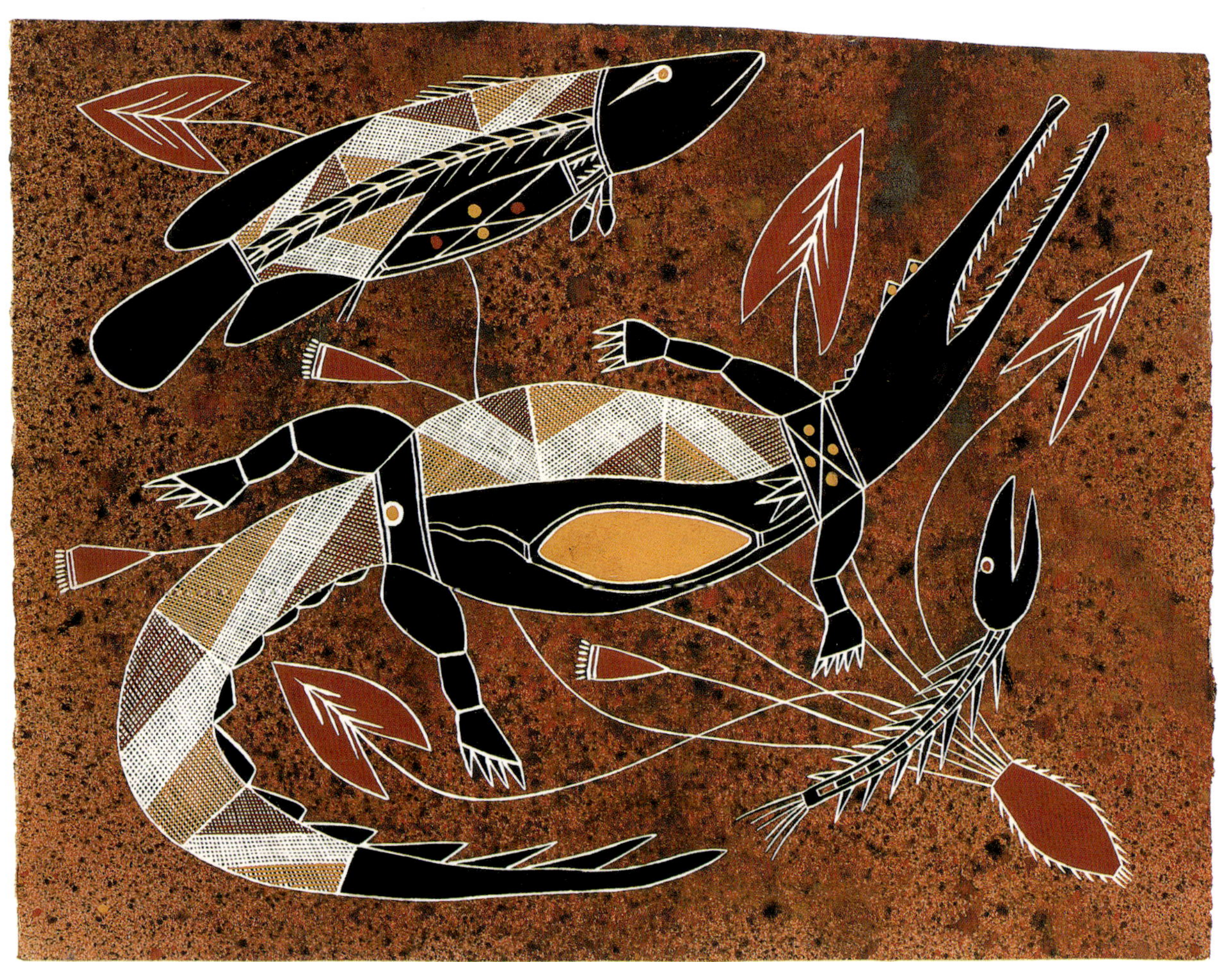

S.H.

Crocodile and Barramundi, *by Joshua Bangar, 60 x 48 cm*

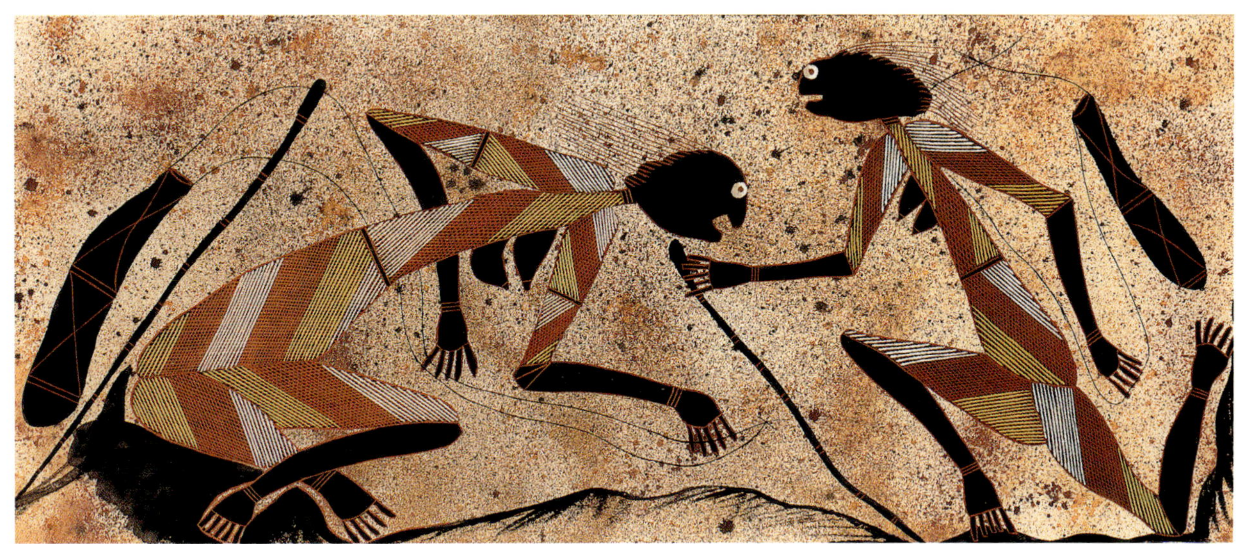

Likanaya and Marrayka, *by Alex Nganjmirra, 110 x 51 cm*

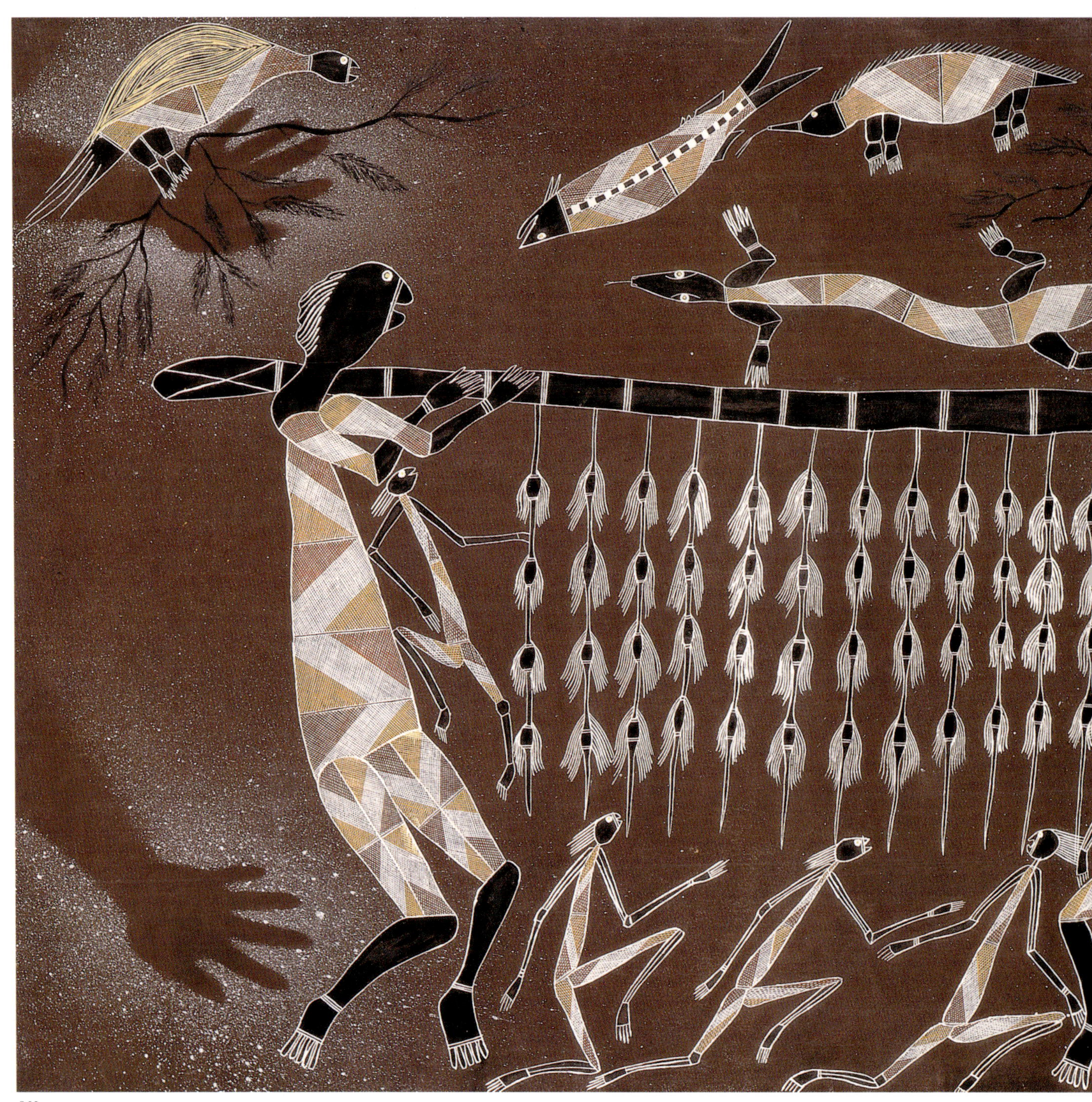

Mardayin Ceremony, *by Alex Nganjmirra, 150 x 102 cm*

That's man, two Binninj people, dancing like Mardayin. Mardayin is for us, Yirridja ceremony.

In this painting two young men are dancing with a hollow log placed between them on their shoulders. Decorating the log are strings of feathers gathered from the parrots represented in the top left and right-hand corners. The dance signals the beginning of the Mardayin ceremony. This dance also tells *Dhuwa* people that it is time to stop hunting and eating their *djang*, animals

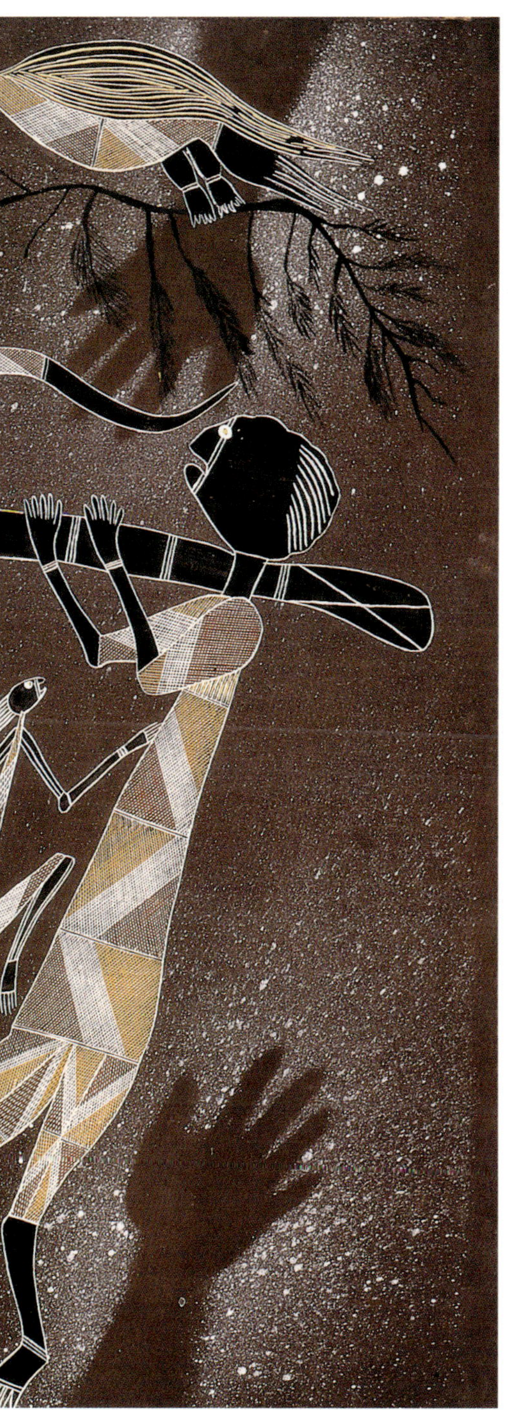

sacred to their skin group. In this instance the animals are saratoga, goanna and echidna. The giant, Luma Luma, taught the Kunwinjku people this ceremony. Around the two young men other *Binninj* people are dancing. Sacred sticks are used during the ceremony. The *Dhuwa* people dance with a fighting stick representing the yam, while the *Yirridja* people dance with a stick representing the long-tom fish.

BELOW: *The pool at Marlwon where the Yawk Yawk sisters emerge to sunbake*

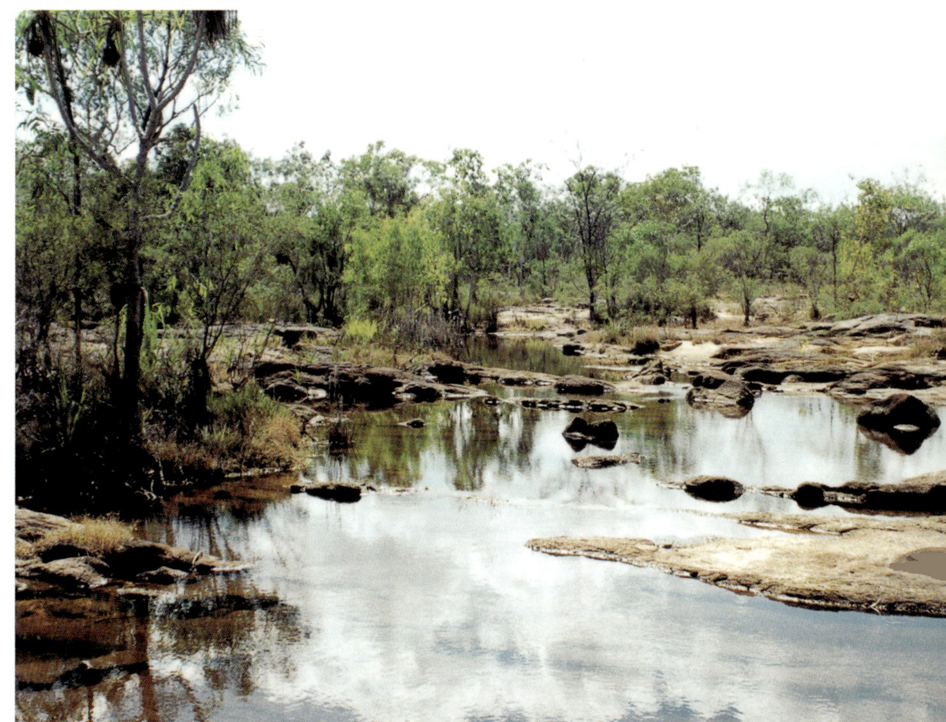

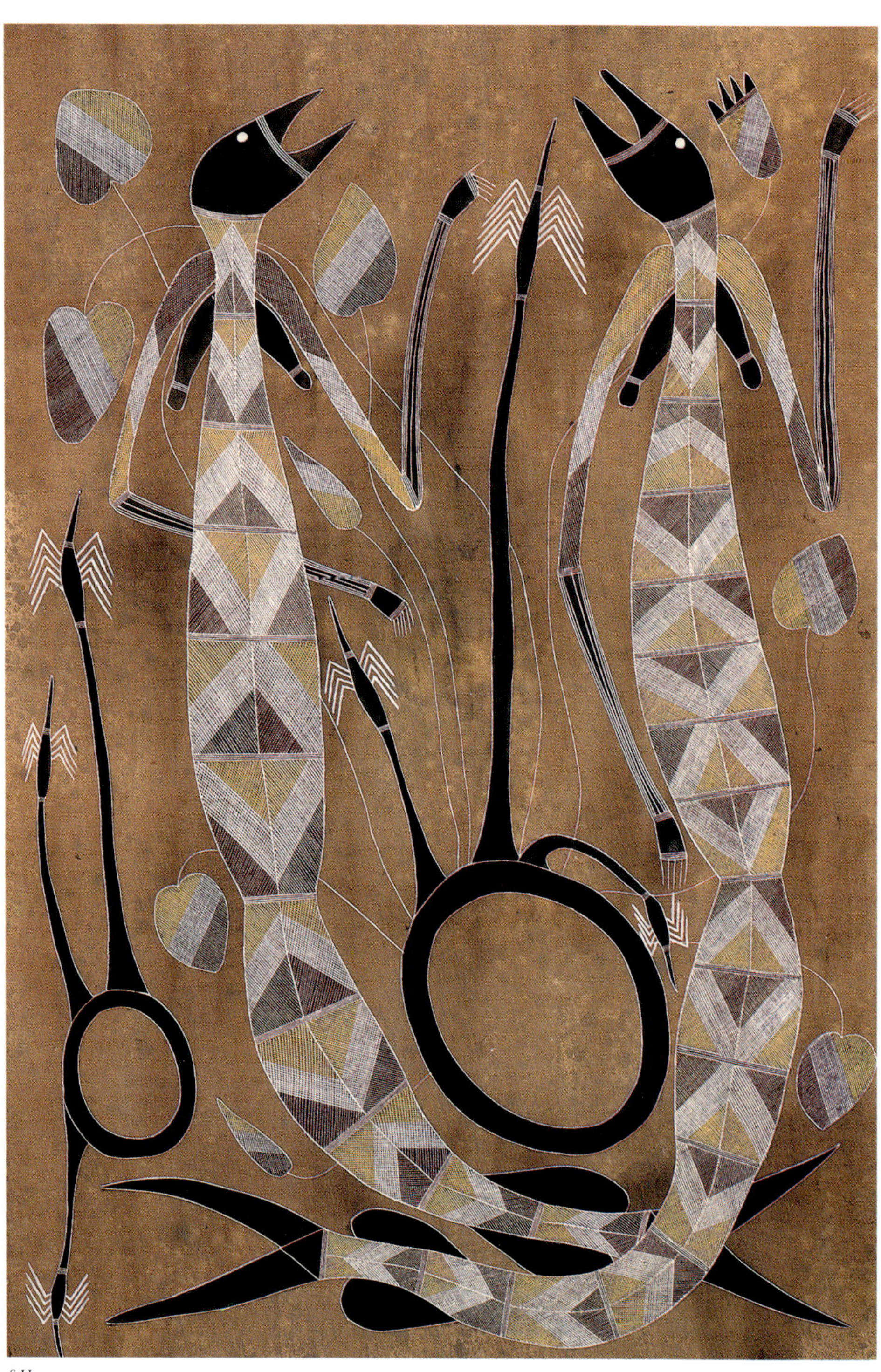

S.H.

Yawk Yawk Sisters, *by Thompson Nganjmirra, 102 x 150 cm*

At Marlwon, downstream from the pool in which the spirits of Marrayka and Likanaya reside, lies another pool which contains the *Yawk Yawk* spirits. At times, when no one is looking, their fish-like tails metamorphose into legs so that they may climb out of the water and sunbathe on the rocks adjacent to Marlwon Creek. The *Yawk Yawk* sisters can also metamorphose into dragonflies.

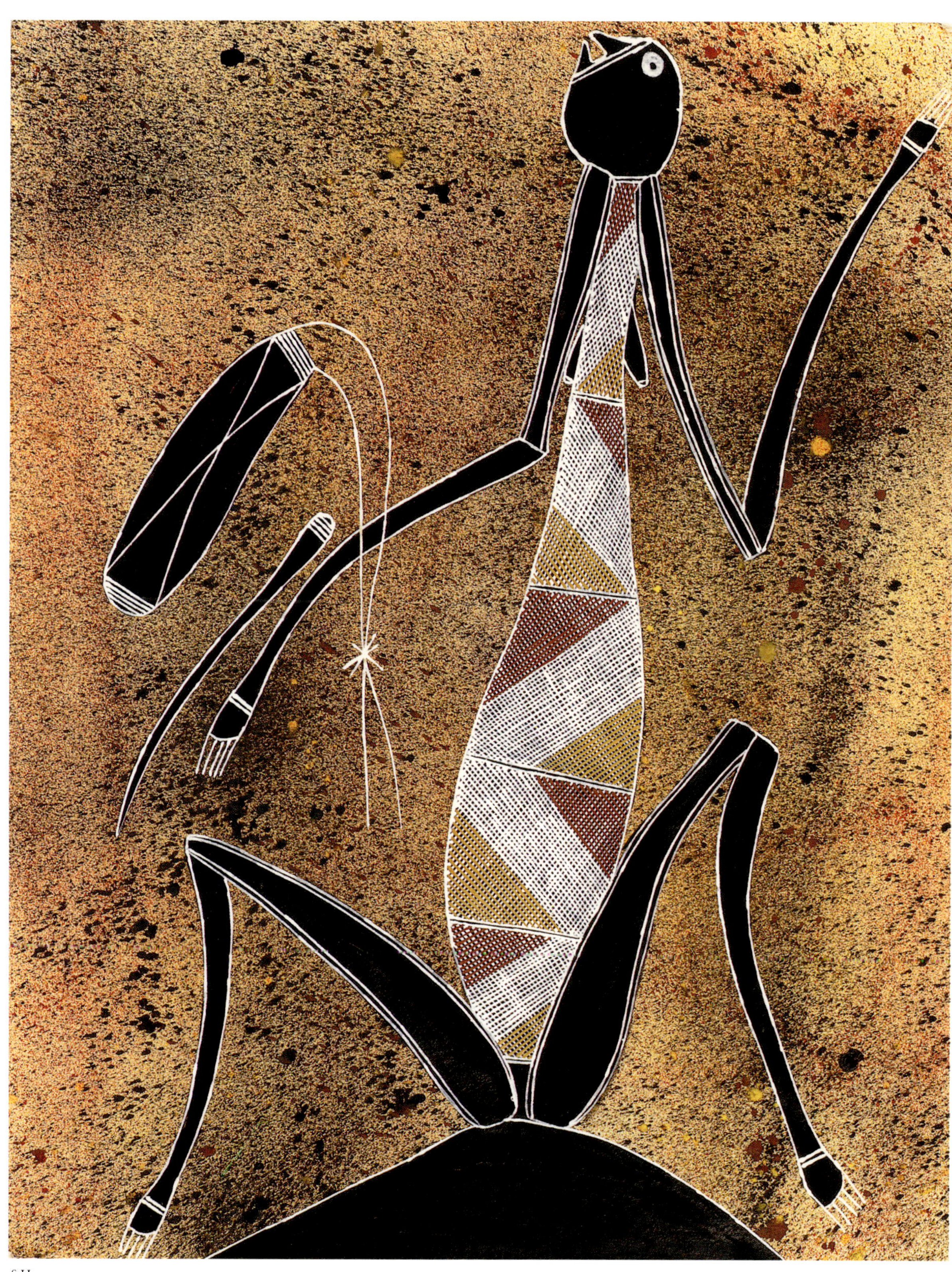

Marrayka, *by Trevor Nganjmirra, 51 x 66 cm*

Here, Marrayka is seen sitting on the water's edge at Marlwon. She has a digging stick and dilly bag.

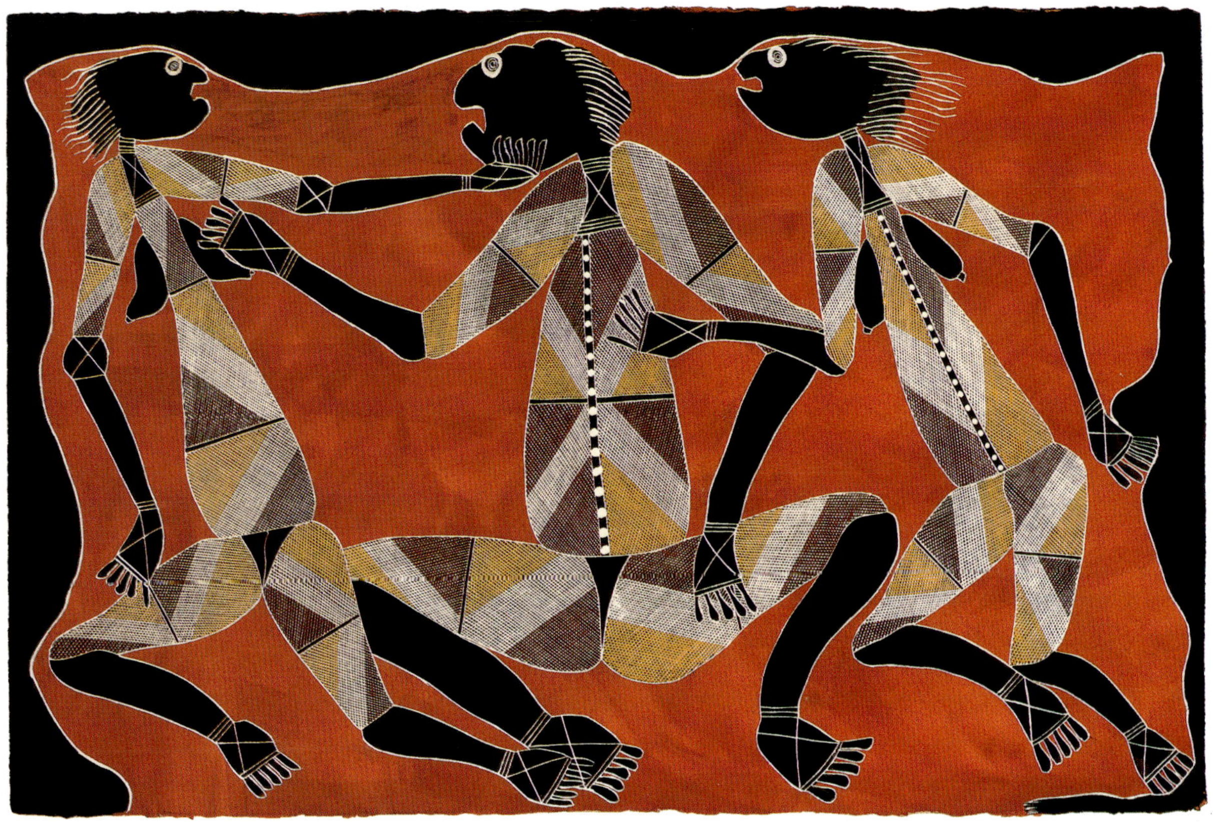

Luma, Marrayka and Ngalkunburriyaymi, *by Alex Nganjmirra, 101 x 66 cm*

In this painting, Marrayka is seducing Luma Luma. Angry and jealous, *Ngalkunburriyaymi*

is attempting to solicit Luma's favour for herself.

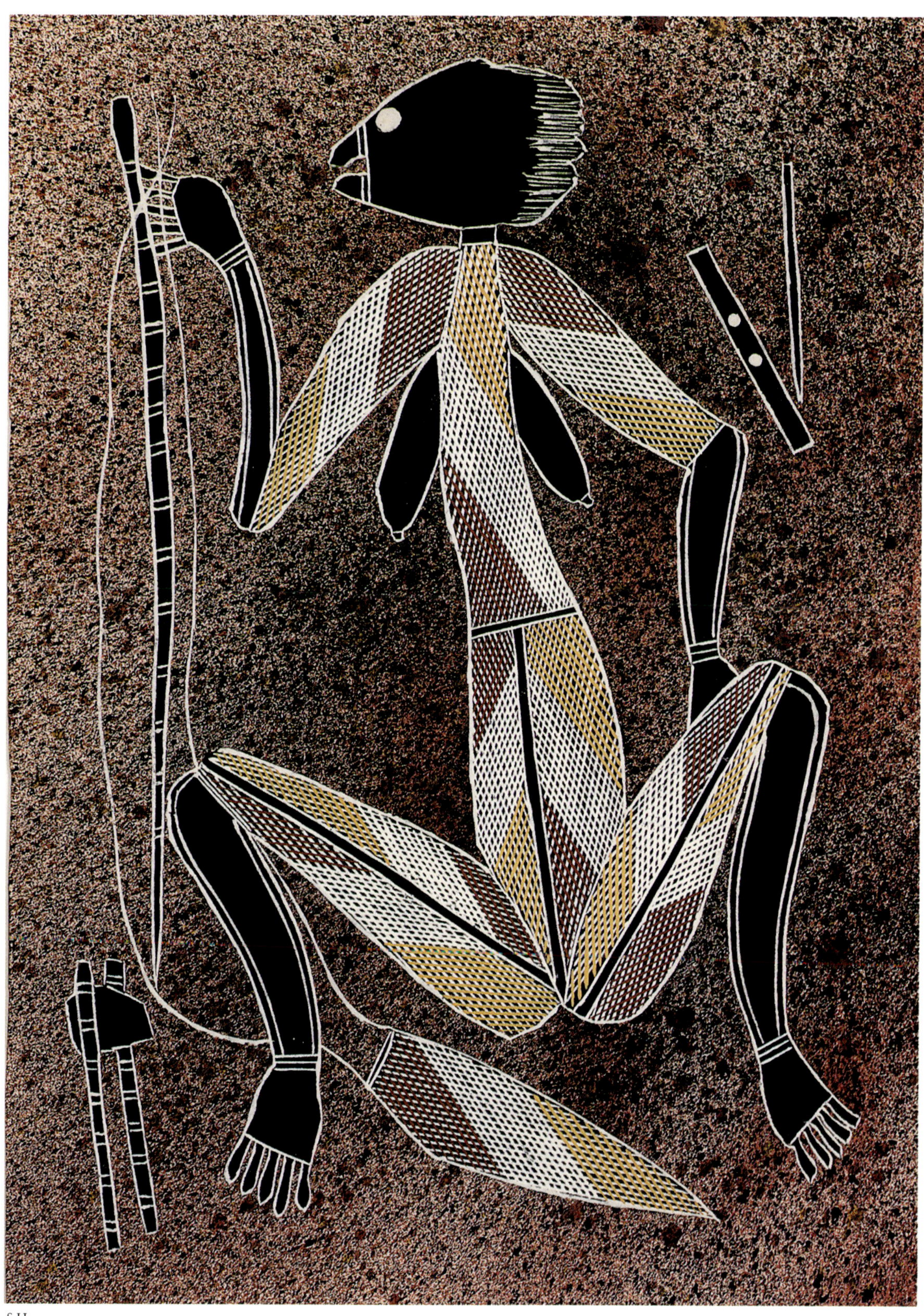

S.H.

Marrayka, *by Alex Nganjmirra, 32 x 48 cm*

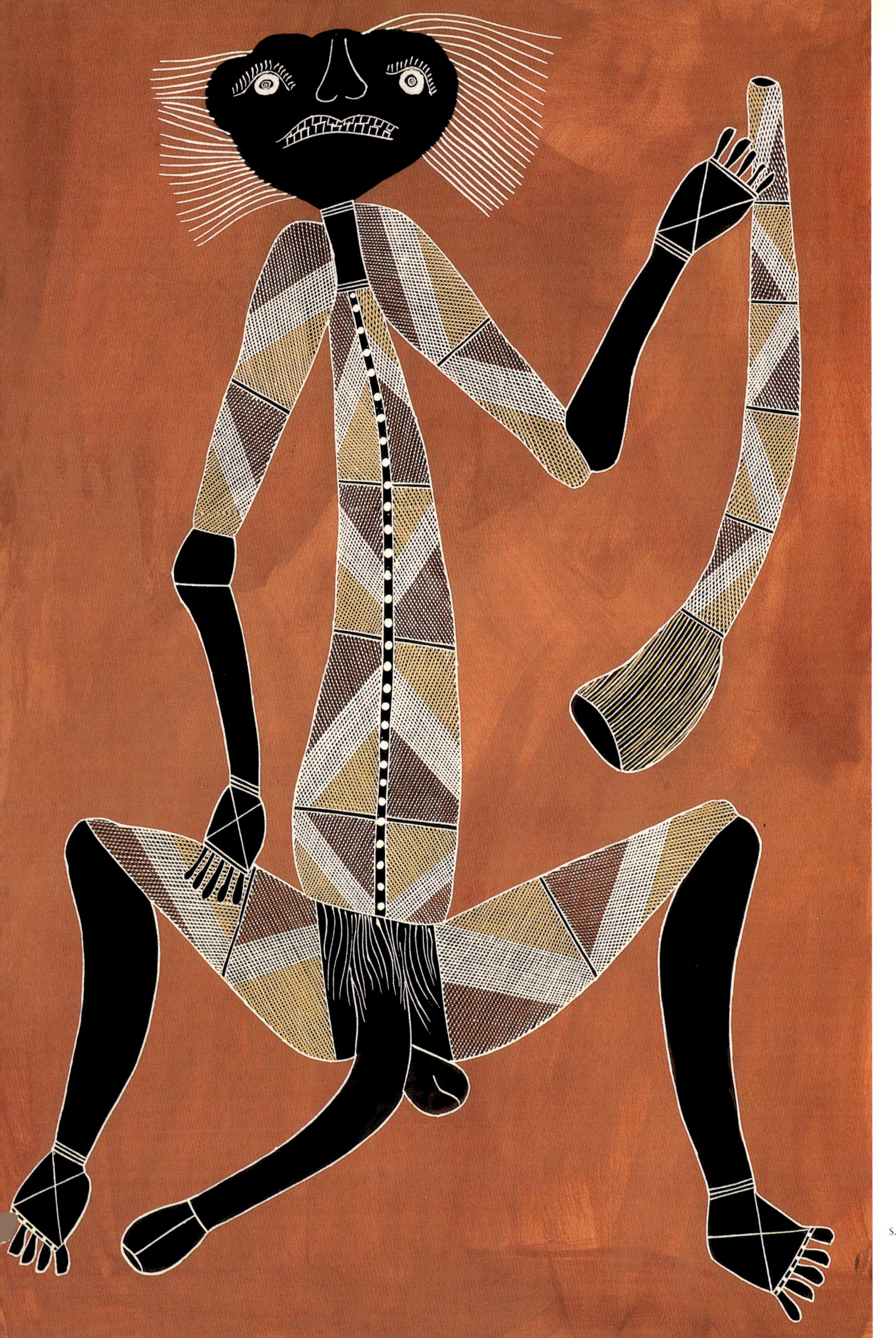

S.H.

The didgeridoo is a central component of Aboriginal life and ceremony in the northern parts of Australia. It can be manufactured and played by men only. Numerous stories throughout northern Australia describe the origin and use of the instrument. Locally, the origins of the didgeridoo are described in the story of Bilk Bilk.

That's Bilk Bilk. You can see that one got the long penis. He went out and used to kill the people. He was bad. So the people they made a little hole in the ground to make him go down, to fall in and then kill him. Get a spear. He was bad guy killing people and raping. He was an angry man. He used to see a girl, he would rape her.

So the people dug the hole, the parents, you know the mother and father, they got a bit upset and all them uncles, cousins, brothers of them girls, the ones he raped, so they angry at Bilk Bilk as he was raping and killing and they dug the hole and told him to come here, come here, more better. So he

Didgeridoos

walked toward them but Bilk Bilk couldn't see the hole, it was a trap. They covered them leaves, you know, leaves to make it so he would reckon it was flat ground, but there was a hole covered with leaves.

Bilk Bilk walked toward the people and then he went down, fell down into the hole. The people they came back and got spear and threw it, speared him, but he didn't die, he was still alive, so he got his dick and cut it off. Made big didgeridoo, that's the one he's holding, didgeridoo. That's his dick. He said, 'I'm still alive, I'm not killed, still alive', so he made that song.

He made that song for us, for everybody he said sing. He blowed and we made ourselves song, for Kunwinjku people and all other people, everybody. After he played the song he died. The men said we go now because he told us we got to look around and make song for them other people. The people went out and look around them tree, them didgeridoo, look around and see if any are hollow and cut it and make a didgeridoo. Bilk Bilk taught the people music. Women are not allowed to play, only for Binninj man, yeah, them dick, not ladies. The women can dance.

Alex Nganjmirra

Bilk Bilk, *by Alex Nganjmirra,*
66 x 101 cm

MANUFACTURE

Didgeridoos are manufactured mostly during the Dry season. Didgeridoos made during the Wet usually split when the water-soaked timber begins to dry. On the other hand, at the end of the Dry, the timber is too hard to fell easily. It is the period between the two seasons (shortly after the burn-offs) that is best for production, while the timber is drying slowly and is easier to cut. During the Wet the dense undergrowth makes bush navigation and walking difficult, but fire management of the land makes vast areas of bush easily accessible. After the burn-off, one can select appropriate didgeridoo trees unhampered.

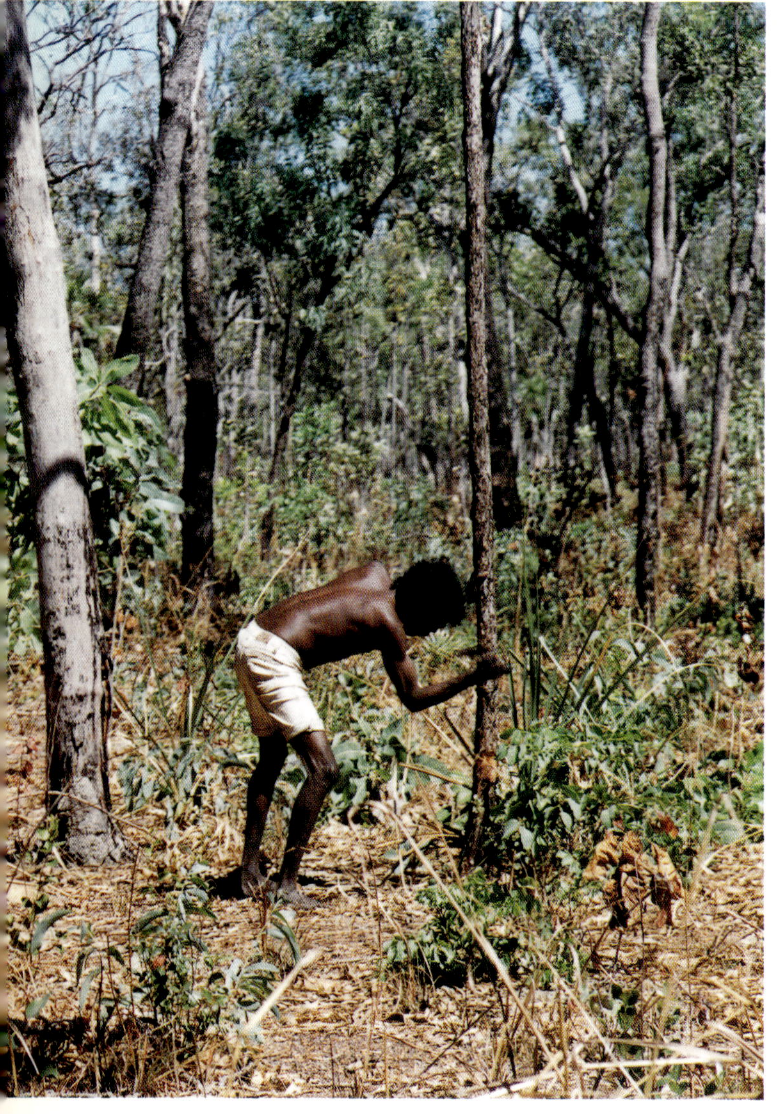

Men are taught the techniques of didgeridoo craftsmanship from a young age. Initially, boys are taught to locate and identify appropriate trees. Later they learn the manufacturing and painting techniques. Central to didgeridoo making is termite activity. Termites are found all over Australia, but in the northern regions they are more abundant and rapacious, building nests up to four metres in height.

Young men are taught to recognise when termite activity is taking place inside a tree. They are taught to read the various visible signs, such as termite dirt on the trunk, or holes on the tree plugged by the termites to prevent exposure to sunlight. Hollow or dying branches are also a positive sign. Usually, saplings rather than the branches of older trees are used to make the instrument. When a tree of the appropriate diameter with visible termite activity is found, it is tested to find out if it is hollow. A knife is used to peel away a small section of bark so that the timber can be tapped or flicked with a finger. If it sounds hollow, a

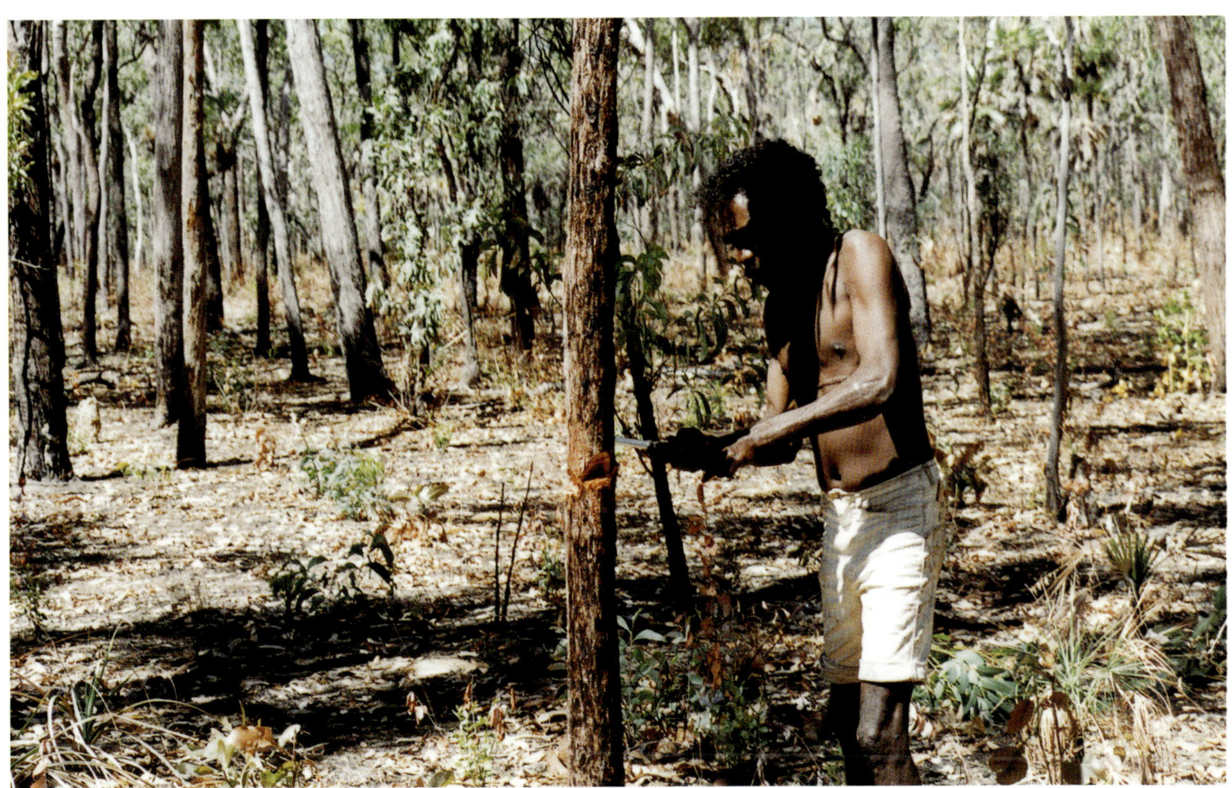

tomahawk is used to cut a small wedge about 30 cm from the base, so that a visual inspection can be made. If the sapling is deemed suitable it is felled. Otherwise it can be left standing; it has not been ringbarked and will continue to grow.

Once felled, the sapling is again tested five to six feet further up the trunk to see if the hollow is long enough. If so, the desired length is cut and the artist has a blank from which he will craft an instrument.

Back at the camp, the remaining termites and termite dirt are removed by pounding the log on the ground. Blockages can be removed by ramming them out with a broom handle or stick. The residue is flushed out with water. The blank is then ready to be debarked.

The bark is stripped with a sharp implement, usually a knife, so that the timber is exposed. A wood rasp is used to file away bark residue and to hone the mouth piece. The blank is then sanded by hand, smoothing it in readiness for painting. This process often exposes small holes in the timber which can

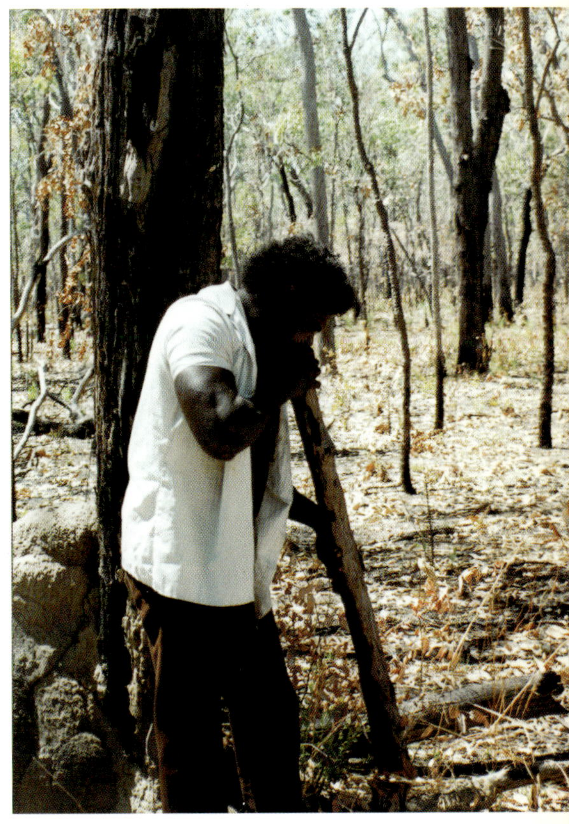

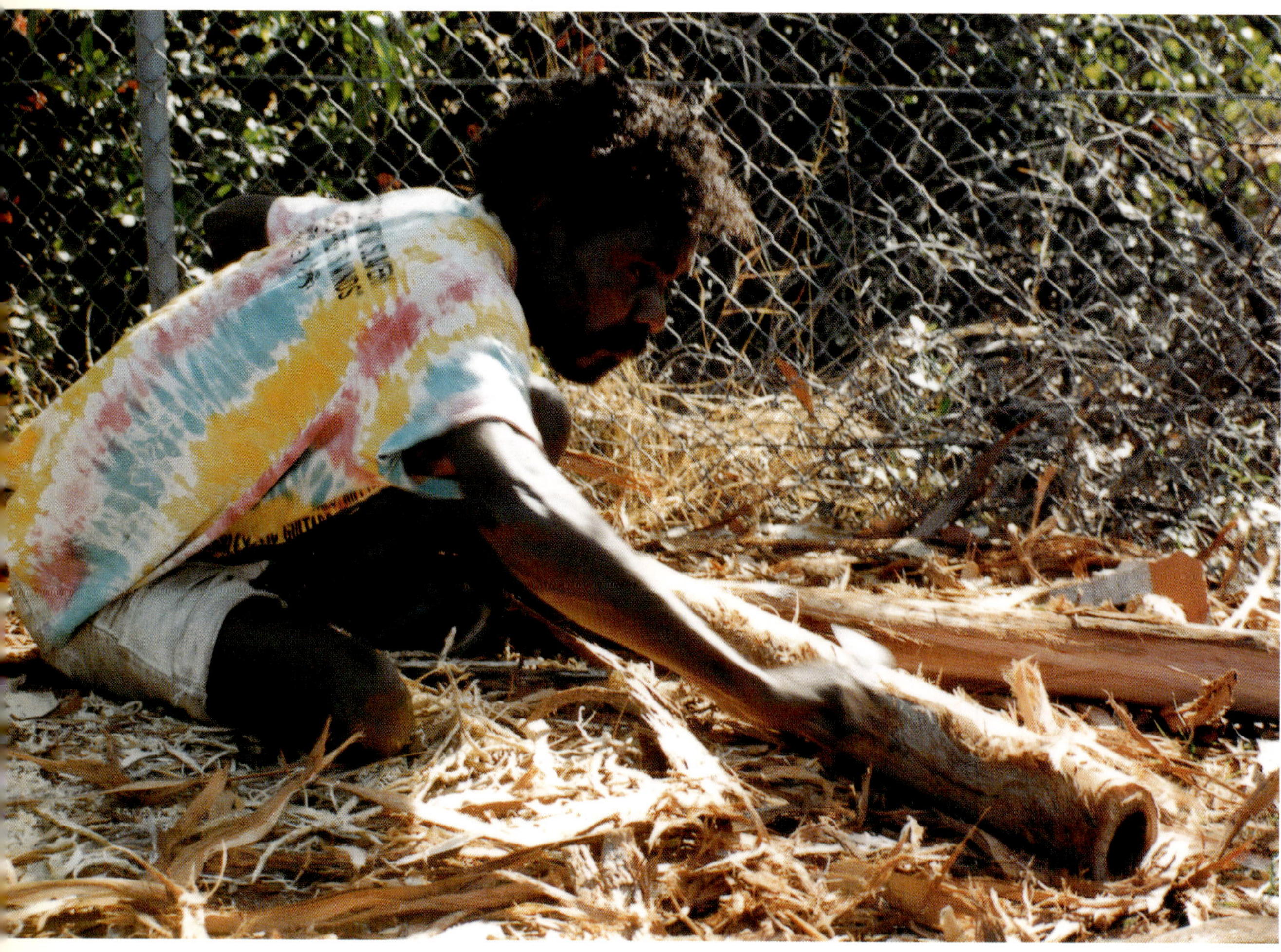

Debarking the blank

be plugged by tapping in small twigs or covered with glued paperbark. Cracks can be sealed with beeswax.

Most didgeridoos are painted, though occasionally they are left blank or inscribed with burnt designs (a recent innovation). The approach to painting a didgeridoo is the same as with work on bark and paper. Foodstuffs and stories feature prominently. However, some didgeridoos are decorated with secret themes of ceremonial importance and can be viewed only by initiated men. It is for ceremony that the instrument is most important. When played it brings the stories of the Dreamtime, hunting and animals to life. It is also commonly used for informal and recreational purposes.

Association with the didgeridoo begins at a young age. Locals believe that if a young man swallows the eggs of a certain type of frog, the ability to play and 'circular breathe' will come naturally. As with any instrument, some players are more outstanding than others. When playing, traditional

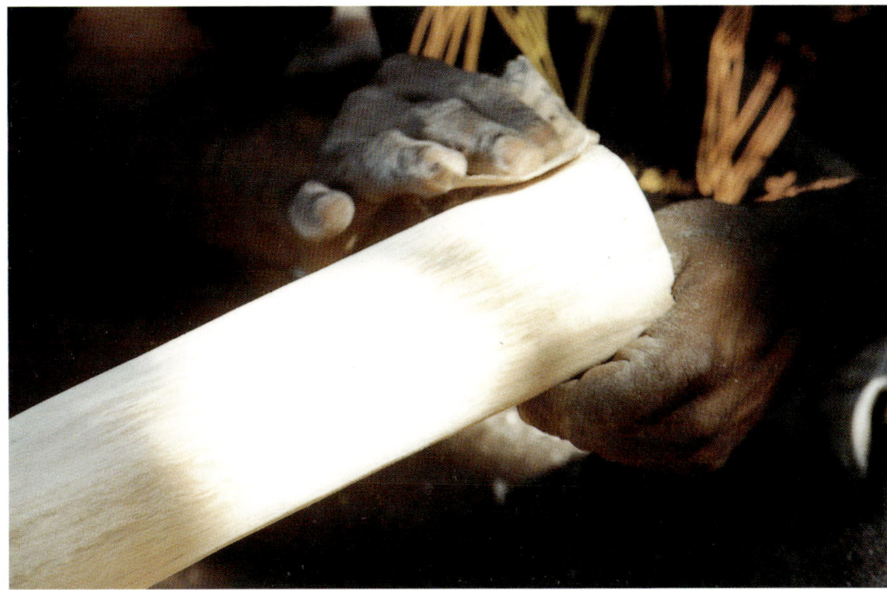

language-based rhythms are used. As with painting and dancing, the young musician is taught particular rhythms and playing techniques. He will rarely venture outside these. Non-traditional rhythms are referred to as contemporary rhythms.

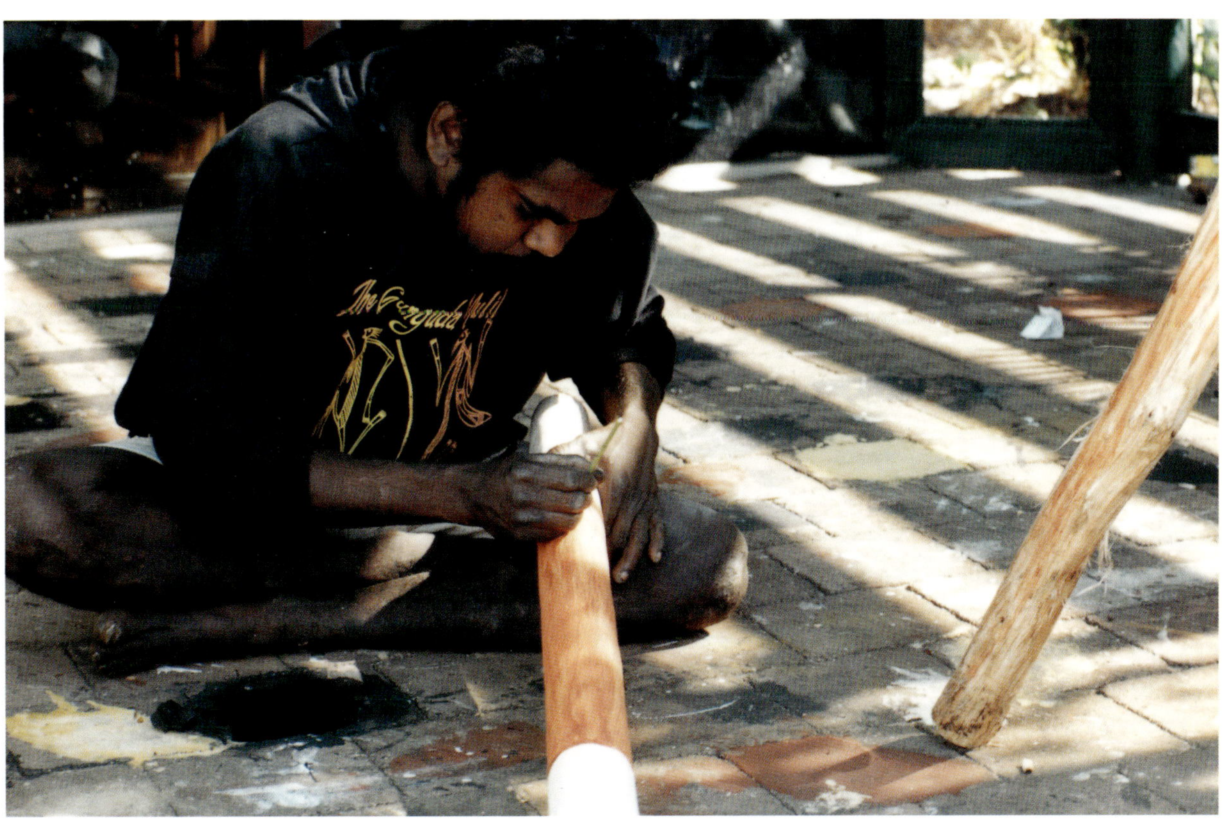

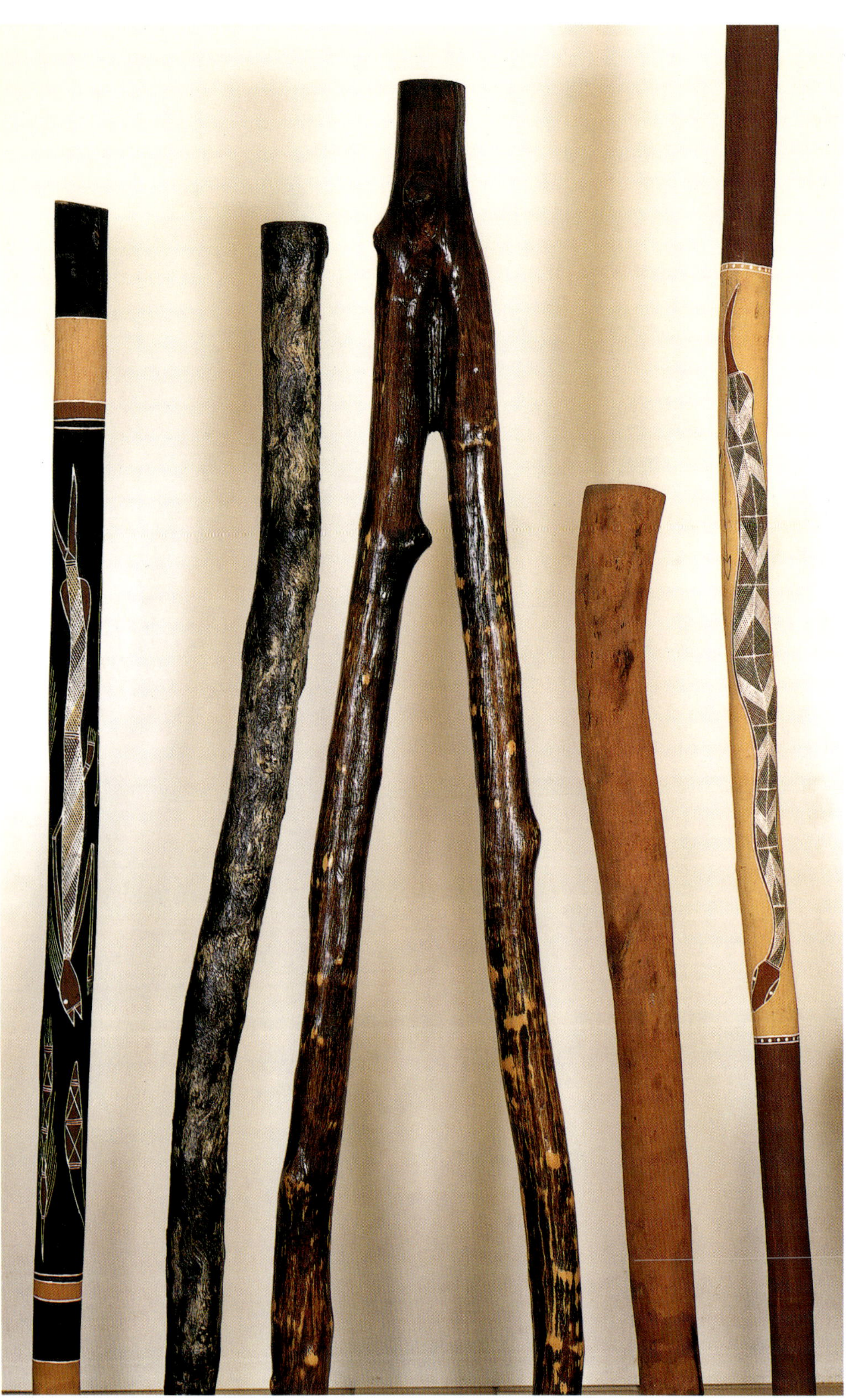

Three blank and two painted didgeridoos, by Joshua Bangar and Chris Ngaboy

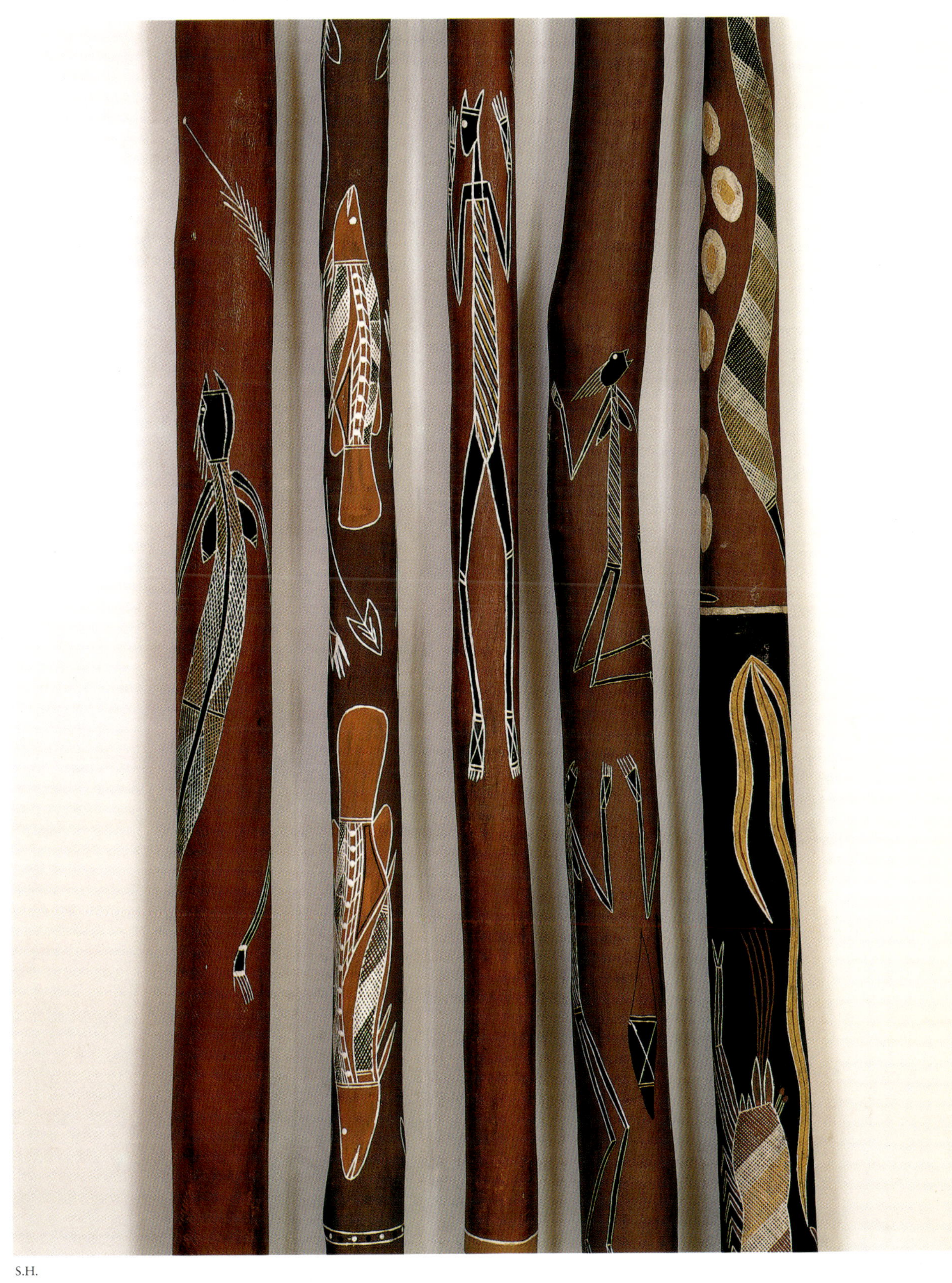

Assorted didgeridoos, by (from left to right) David Cameron, Chris Ngaboy, David Cameron, Chris Ngaboy, Mark Nadjongorle

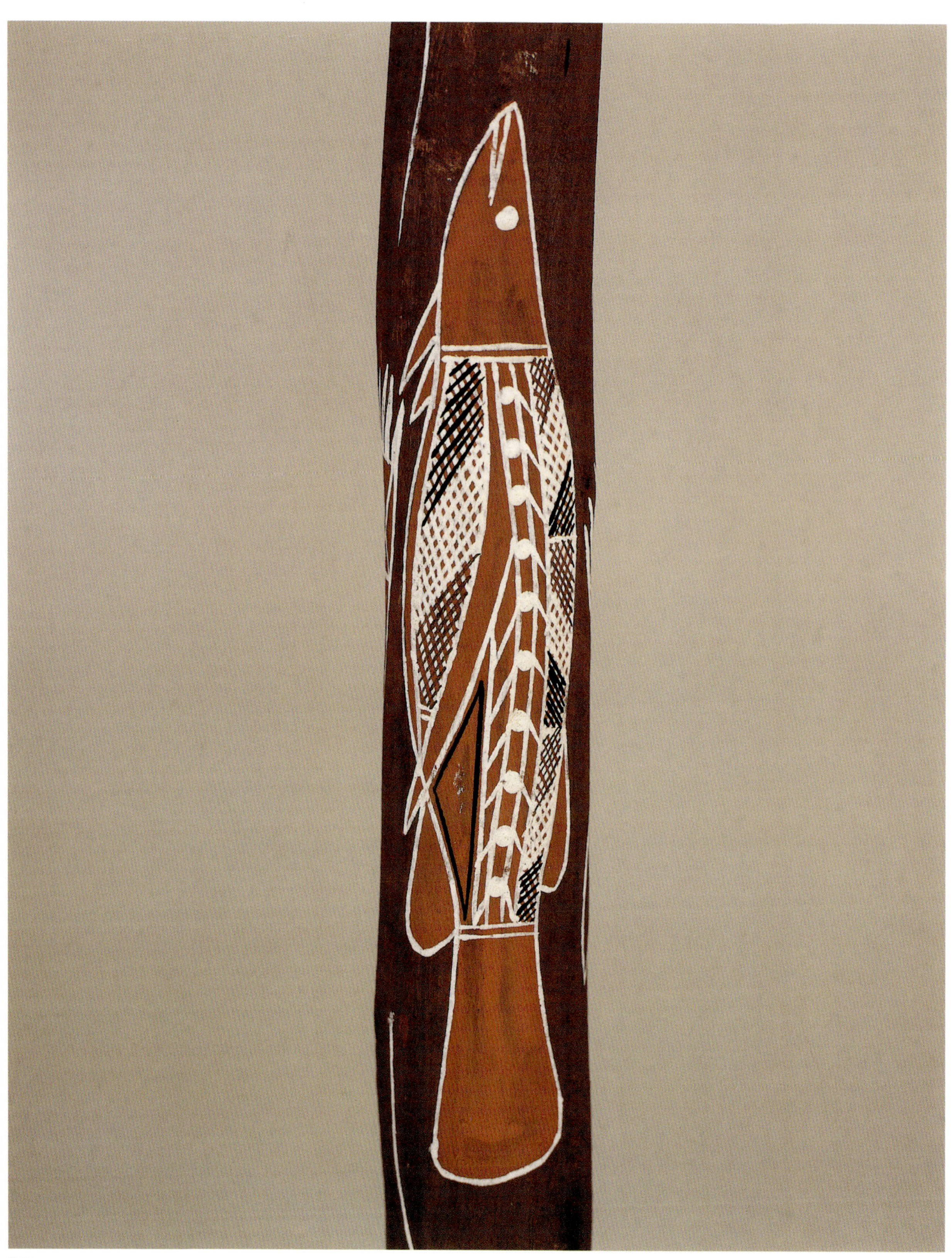

S.H.

Detail of didgeridoo, by Chris Ngaboy

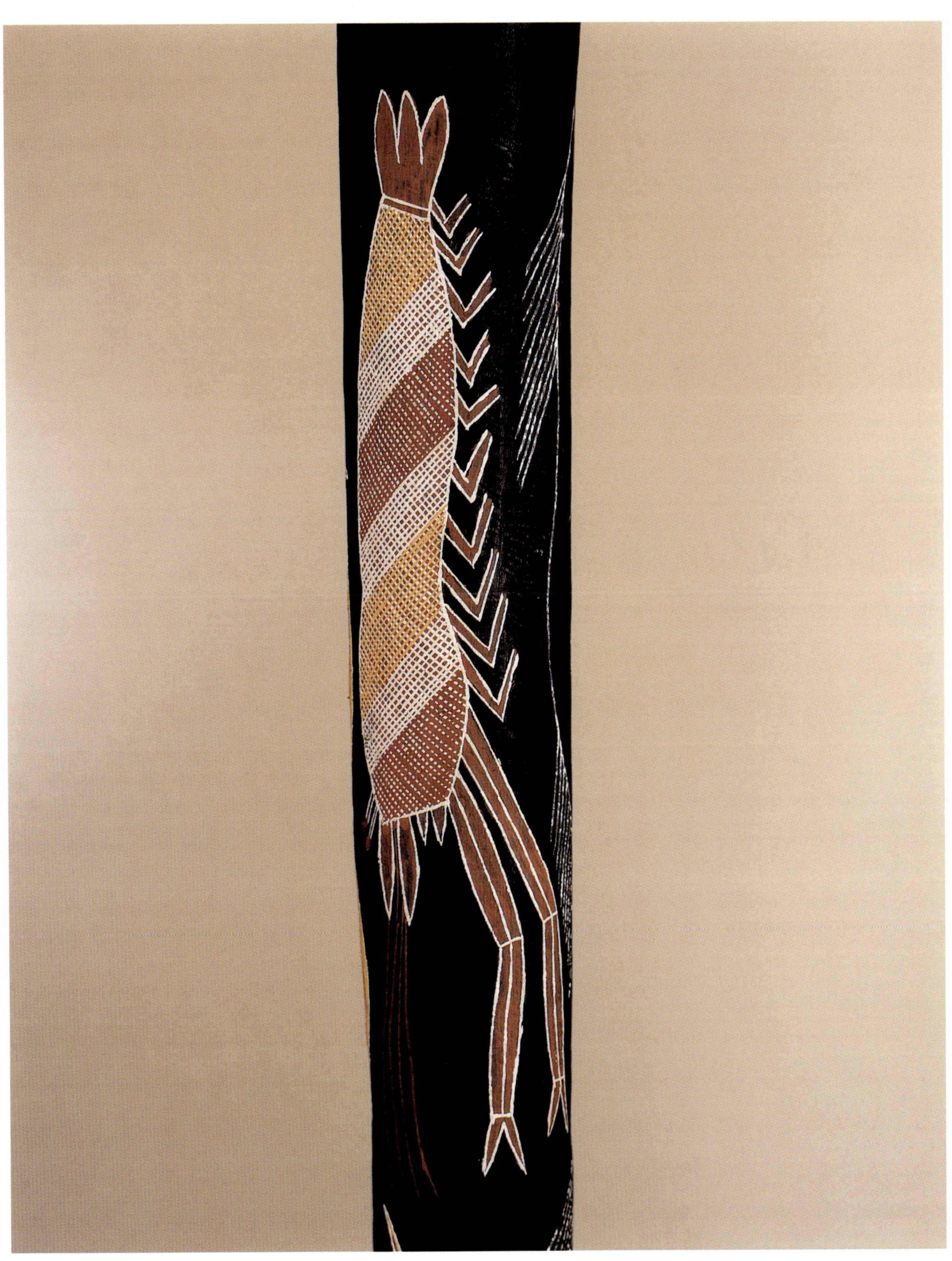

Detail of didgeridoo, by David Cameron

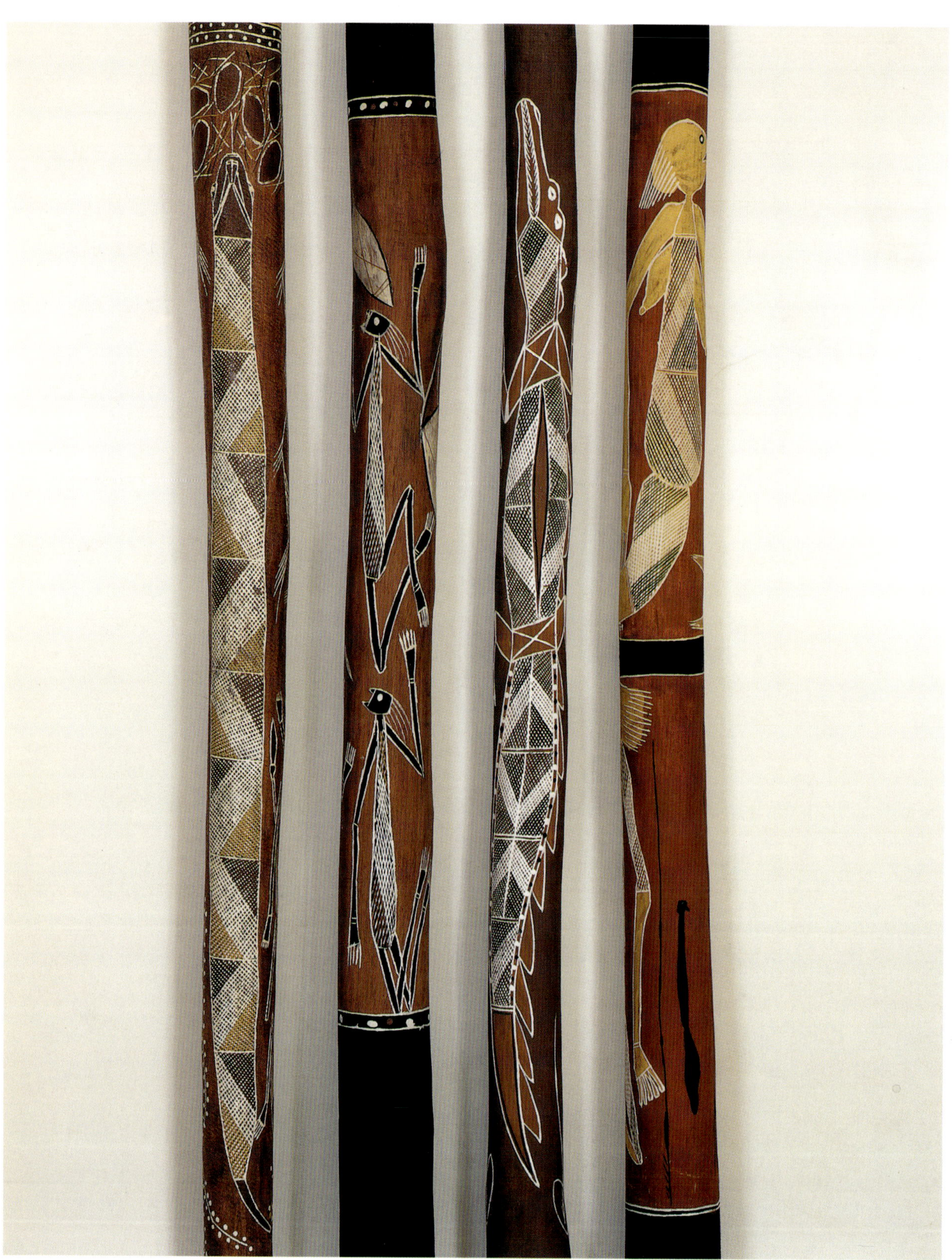

S.H.

Assorted didgeridoos, by (from left to right), Alex Nganjmirra, Chris Ngaboy, Mark Nadjongorle, Chris Ngaboy

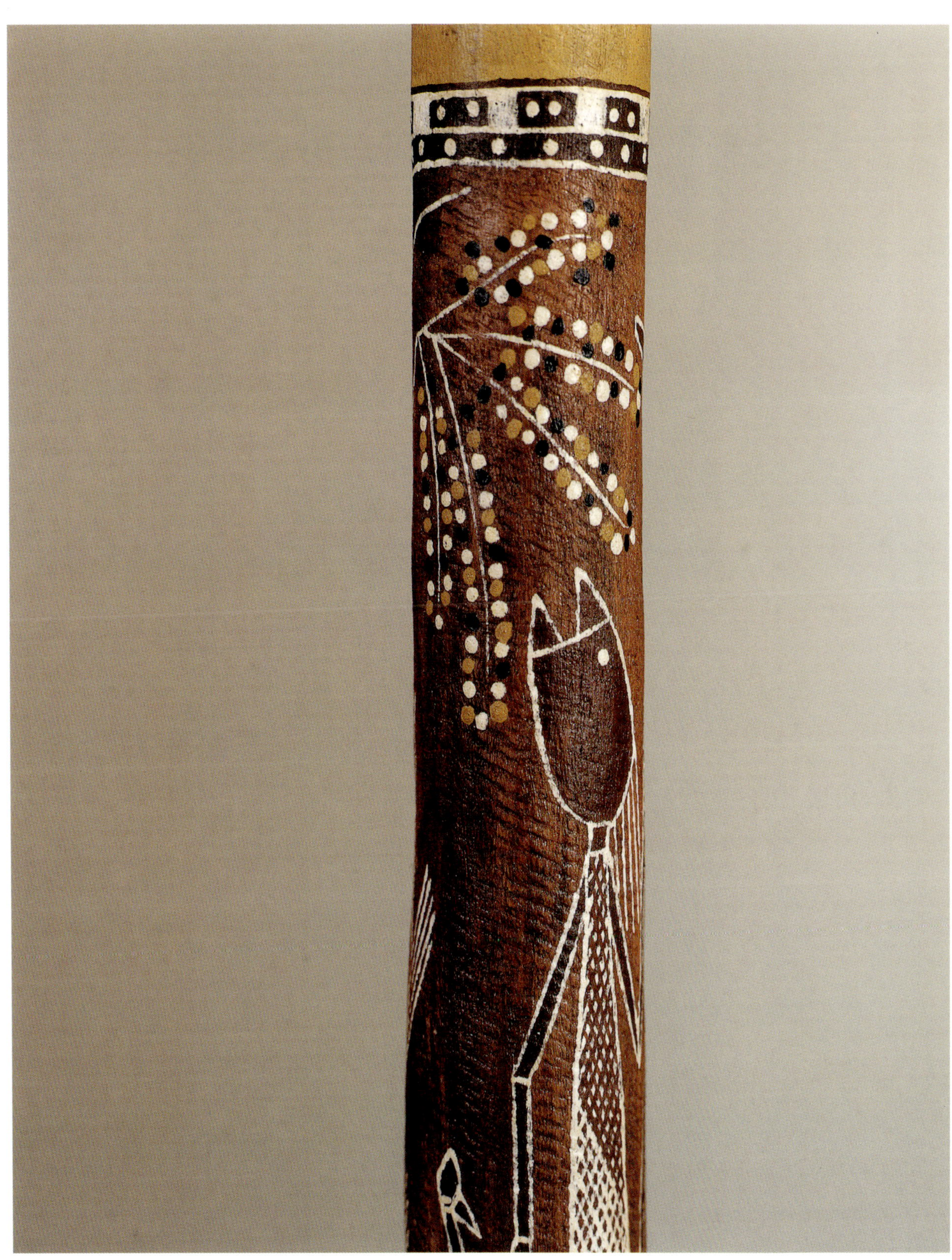

S.H.

Detail of didgeridoo, by Chris Ngaboy

Index